THE LONELY SOLDIER:
The War Memoirs of a Polish Partisan.

THE LONELY SOLDIER:
The War Memoirs of a Polish Partisan.

Z. W. Maslany

With Jeremy Huxley Ward

CALIBAN BOOKS

© Caliban Books
First Published 1989
by Caliban Books
17 South Hill Park Gardens
Hampstead, London NW3

ISBN 1 85066 008 5

Typset by ImagePlus, Lewes, East Sussex

Printed and bound in Great Britain by
BPCC Wheatons Ltd, Exeter

CONTENTS

Page Number

THE LONELY SOLDIER.

Introduction by J. H. Ward.

When Mr. Maslany (whom I always knew as 'Jan', his wartime pseudonym) first sent his manuscript in to Caliban Books, I was asked to give my opinion of it by Peter Razzell, the managing director of Caliban. We found that our thoughts on it coincided, namely that while it was completely unpublishable as it stood, there was the potential of a very interesting book in the making. One of the problems was that Jan had never written a book before; the other was that although his English was very good, it was not his first language.

We wrote to him and a week or so later, we met "Jan" in person; he turned out to be a large, energetic, a very physical kind of man, looking rather older than his years. At the time we met, he had been temporarily crippled by a fall caused by an icy road, which had smashed his hip. Ironic that after so many adventures, and so many hair-raising dangers, such a minor accident should cause damage where Hitler's and Stalin's armies had failed.

It was agreed that I should work with him as co-author and editor, arranging the material which he provided, and re-writing it as necessary. For a time the work went well, but after a time we began to run into difficulties. There was plenty of material available, that was obvious: but most of it had been left out of the original manuscript. He constantly mentioned fascinating stories or incidents which remained half told. When I pressed for details, he became distinctly distressed, as if the whole matter was very painful to him. At one point, when he remembered the woman spy with whom he became sexually and romantically involved, and who was poisoned in front of him, he began crying. It was very seldom one sees a man crying – and only the fact that I have a number of friends in the "therapy" movement, and have some experience in this area, prevented me from becoming very embarrassed.

As time went on, it became more and more obvious that the book was far more important to Jan than a book generally is to an author. Through it, he was trying to purge himself finally of the horrors of an experience which had remained long buried.

However, he remained very hard to press on these points. And I found that the only way to talk to him was through taking him for a drink. After a few vodkas, he became more talkative, and sometimes began to talk about the buried incidents – many involving acts of extreme violence – but very frequently he found himself unable to continue, having great difficulty in remembering these incidents in detail. Since his memory for so much of his war experience was so good, it was obvious that these lapses of memory were some kind of unconscious defence mechanism.

I found that by degrees, I was becoming his therapist, although that was not our formal relationship. But it became more and more clear that he was going through some kind of therapeutic experience in re-discovering the terrible things that he had seen, suffered, and perhaps most important of all, had himself perpetrated.

I went so far as to seek advice from an experienced therapist whom I happened to know; his advice was not to encourage the emotional outbursts, but not to discourage or disapprove of them in any way.

This was not always easy; when Jan was drunk, he did not always behave well, and on at least one occasion, was thrown out by the landlord. However, we made progress, and slowly I found out the details, not only of his adventures, but of the mental difficulties which had plagued him, the terrible dreams and disturbed sleep from which he had suffered for many years after the war.

One problem remained persistent in our work. Jan's memory for detail was good, and became clearer all the time as he talked. But he never described, and indeed could not describe, his reactions to his experiences. One reader who saw an early draft said: "It is as if it were happening to somebody else."

I talked to Jan about this, and he explained that people who felt the emotional impact of the terrible things that were going on during the war could not carry on, and perished. The person who felt was the person who died.

No doubt that was true – but it was far from being the whole story. The fact was that Jan had never, even afterwards, felt the whole emotional impact of what he went through; he could not bear to, even in the quiet surroundings of seaside Bournemouth, where he lived. And even as he talked and wrote, even then the emotions that were aroused could not fully surface; for all the tears and misery the memories aroused, they were still censored. The emotional suppression which had become a habit in the war had become a lifelong, and very unhealthy, habit, and had taken a very heavy toll of Jan's post-war years.

One thing that did come over, however, and that was Jan's complete truthfulness – for it obviously cost him so much to tell what he did. It often cost me a lot of digging to get at the more unpleasant details; for example, the torture and rape of prisoners he witnessed while with the Italian partisans. He would have preferred me to concentrate on such things as the details of his engineering work for the German army, work which was of little general interest. Indeed, while I was writing the book, one friend to whom I mentioned it suggested that Jan was making it all up. I told him that, apart from the authentication I had managed to obtain, such an idea was laughable. If Jan had had his way, we would have published a very dull book indeed, and many of the more interesting events would have remained forever buried.

Not that we have not sought authentication – indeed, we went to great lengths in this respect. Firstly, we obtained Jan's war record from the Polish Institute's archives in this country. I also met personally Roman Zagurski, Jan's oldest friend, who was with him in the Russian prisoner of war camp and who met him in Italy when he was with the partisans.

We also obtained a letter from the person who appears in the book as "Omar", and who was Jan's commander during the period when he fought with the partisans. We had a curious experience with this man. We sent him a translation of the chapters of the book which deal with Italy, the chapters in which he appears; he appears under a pseudonym, on account of the fact that these partisan days are still, in Italy, a matter of great political sensitivity.

He returned us a letter saying that of couse he had no personal knowledge of these matters, but he was sure that Jan spoke the truth. A contradiction in terms, since the book described him as having very definite personal knowledge of the matters described. However, apparently there is still such feeling about those days, when Italian often fought Italian, and when Communist partisans sometimes crossed with non-Communist fighters, that 'Omar' did not dare to say more.

The main area we wished to check, however, were his wartime intelligence missions; which form the backbone of the book. The first step was to try to find details of the intelligence unit with which "Jan" served. To this end, we wrote to the Ministry of Defence and to archive sources in America, all to no purpose. Everyone denied knowledge of any Allied unit which used Polish agents.

We wrote many letters to experts in wartime and intelligence history; most of them were unable to help. But one, Mr. James

Rusbridger, pointed out, vis a vis intelligence operations in the Middle East during World War II, that "many . . . were of a very ad hoc nature, and run without any official authorisation,"

Some general confirmation of this came in IN THE SECRET SERVICE by General Rygor Slovikowski. In this book, Slovikowski lays bare the way in which the Americans exploited Polish intelligence gathered by the Free Polish Army in North Africa, and used it without giving credit to the Poles. This did not confirm Jan's involvement, but it gave some explanation for the brick wall we had come up against.

In the course of my inquiries, I contacted a man famous in his own right – one Eddie Chapman, himself a double agent during the Second World War. He was most friendly and helpful, and made enquiries among his many friends in the intelligence community.

He provided one key piece of information – an unconfirmed report that an English officer, one Colonel Slade-Baker, had run an intelligence unit which had operated out of Beirut, on behalf of the Americans. Jan had previously told us that one of his superior officers was a Colonel Slade, who had operated out of Egypt.

Search of the Army lists of the time revealed a Colonel John Bigelow Slade-Baker, of the Royal Army Ordnance Corps. During the war, he had not been with his unit, however, but had been officially attached to the British Military Mission to the Egyptian Army from 2/9/39 to 30/11/42, after which he seems to have had no special duties, being merely listed as Lt. Col. in the Royal Army Ordnance Corps – a bland anonymity which would have fitted in with some kind of secret appointment. After the war, he had worked in the Middle East for the Sunday Times as a correspondent, and had been an expert on Middle Eastern affairs.

The Egyptian posting certainly placed him in the right area; but further enquiries with the Ministry of Defence, with the Colonel's old regiment, and other sources, were all negative – the Colonel had no known connection with intelligence.

It was through the help of Philip Knightley, of the Sunday Times, that we found the book PHILBY; THE LONG ROAD TO MOSCOW, by Patrick Seale and Maureen McConville (Hamish Hamilton 1973), where we found a picture of Colonel Slade-Baker chatting to Kim Philby. Mr. Knightley stated that there was no doubt that the Colonel had been involved in intelligence. He also read our book and is on record as saying that he found it both convincing and important as a study of the realities of war.

Meanwhile I showed the picture of Slade-Baker to Jan – and Jan recognised his old commanding officer – not the man immediately in charge of himself personally, who was Polish, or the English Special

Branch Inspector, Inspector Slack, who ranked above the Pole, but the mysterious higher officer who had commanded the whole unit, and whom he had seen from time to time. This man would turn up, be treated with deference, and look over the intelligence personnel, and then leave. He always wore military uniform without insignia of rank.

The details of Jan's wartime intelligence missions are, of course, ultimately uncheckable by their very nature, but we have enough proof of his wartime record to know that he was a very unusual young soldier, and fought a strange and peculiar war – this, combined with our personal knowledge of him has enabled us to place this record before the public in the confidence that it is true, though, as we have said, some names have had to be changed, at Jan's insistence, to protect people who might be harmed by their disclosure. One of the most important of these is "Engineer Terjung," the German officer who befriended him. Engineer Terjung's past is long behind him, and he cannot afford to be even remotely associated with the Nazis any more, hence the change.

I feel this book is probably unique, and particularly valuable in that it tells the story of war as it is seldom shown – as a terrible traumatic event in which each side does horrible things (whatever the official record may say). It also makes clear that war leaves psychological as well as physical casualties behind; and also it underlines the political cynicism that makes a mockery of the heroism of the average man – as in the meeting which closes this book, in which Marshal Anders, the leader of the free Polish forces, hears that his country has been handed over – bound hand and foot – to Stalin's Russia. How ironic, when one considers that Britain was drawn into the war to defend Poland's liberty; and then co-operated in destroying that same liberty.

But apart from that, above all, the book shows what a terrible and destructive phenomenon violence is: The violence unleashed by the Russians against their Polish prisoners of war; the brutality of the Germans against anybody who opposed them, and the hatred of the partisans towards all Germans. The book does not just show violence in an abstract way but details it in all its nightmarish qualities. For example, the maltreatment of the two German nurses by the partisans as described in this book must be one of the most horrific accounts of human brutality to have been published. And although the author substantially dissociates himself from this violence, he himself commits acts which later make him uneasy and ashamed. For example, there is the German soldier who begged for his life in vain – Jan says that that man's eyes always haunted him afterwards.

One of the most harrowing things about the book is the way that war licences ordinary people, people who we would all see as civilised and sane, to commit the most terrible acts. The men who repeatedly raped the two German nurses were giving vent, not only to their hatred of Germans, but also, I suspect, to their usually deeply repressed hatred of women.

Jan's nightmares after the war persisted for seventeen years; seventeen years during which he awakened, screaming, every night. These were not about the violence inflicted on him, but the violence he had inflicted on others – the German soldier who begged and screamed for his life, the four young Italian women he shot during the swimming incident, and the countless others killed during the ordinary processes of war. Jan's "loneliness" came not only from the effect of the war on him, but because of the terrible violence buried in him, and unleashed by the circumstances of the war; triggered in the end by a confrontation with a fellow prisoner. By talking and writing about this violence, Jan has partly come to terms with what was done to him and what he did to others, though perhaps it is never possible to ever fully come to terms with such terrible and extreme acts of cruelty, whether suffered or inflicted.

One thing is certain; this book should provide a very useful antidote to all those who hold a glorious and romantic view of war and the violence associated with it.

To conclude: I feel I have been really privileged to help Jan with this work – it has certainly broadened my experience, and I would have been much the poorer if he had not written to us. In spite of the difficulties involved in writing the book, and in our work together (and there were quite a few!) I am happy to have done it, and glad to have met Jan and to have him as a friend.

Jeremy H. Ward.

Chapter 1

EARLY YEARS

I was born in Przemysl, in Poland, on 19th June 1924. The first thing I remember was a big fire in the slaughterhouse at the end of the street in the winter of 1928. From what I learnt in later years, 1928 was the severest winter for decades. The snow had reached half way up the ground floor windows and the roads were choked with snow, empty of traffic. Only the railways continued running.

I remember that just before the snow came, the Electric Company had installed a lamp post just across the road - the first one in the locality. It stood in front of a largish building where a tailor worked. Sometimes the whole family would sit and watch him sewing suits. When he was finished, he would always take a huge cast iron from the large coal burning stove he had, and press the suits.

In 1929 my brother and I went to play behind the hospital, which was only two hundred yards away. At the back of the slaughterhouse and across the road was a large field and alongside the road ran a high tension electric power cable, which was suspended from wooden poles. Suddenly, there was a loud banging noise - one of the cables had fallen to the ground. My brother Ted, who was eighteen months older than myself, ran and caught hold of it.

The next thing I remember was him flying through the air, still holding onto the cable; when he hit the ground the cable flew away from him, and he started to cry. I was in a panic; running to him, I saw that his right arm seemed very dirty - in fact, he had suffered an electric burn from the cable, but of course I did not know that. We walked home, my brother screaming with pain. My mother panicked when she saw him, and I got a few smacks on the bottom just for being the uninjured one, though it was in no way my fault! I was really too young to understand what had happened - even when I saw him later in the hospital. However, he recovered well, and his arm only had a slight scar to show what had happened - he was really very lucky.

It is time to introduce us all properly. We were a large family; it consisted of my father, mother, elder brother Ted, myself Zdislaw, my sisters Janina, Lucy, Anna and Irene. The eldest of my sisters was Janina, and she was actually my parents' fourth child - there was a baby who would have been the first child, older than all of us, a girl. However, she only lived for six months after she was born in 1921, and even now I do not know what name they gave her. Janina started Elementary School in 1930 while we lived in Chyrow; there was a strong tie between her and me. There were no secrets between us, and we told each other everything, good and bad; and she often asked my advice as being her elder brother; the trust between us was one hundred per cent.

Lucy was born in 1927. She was the odd one of the family, and had the look of a gypsy, with slightly darker skin than the rest of us. We always used to laugh and say she was the daughter of the chimney sweep. She took her primary education in Chyrow, and then in Zimna Woda till the outbreak of war. Like all of us she was well educated, and eventually she became a teacher in a college of higher education. She is now no longer with us, for she died in November 1985, leaving behind a husband and four grown up children who were very fond of her.

Anna, the next sister, was born in 1929 at Przemysl a few months before we all moved to Chyrow; she is still alive and well and has two children. She has married twice and is still with her second husband. After her comes Irene, who was born in 1932 in Chyrow.

My least favourite relative has always been my dear brother Ted. After the incident at Premysl, from which, as I said, he made a good recovery, he became my mother's 'pet' about the time we moved to Chyrow; goodness knows why. Anyway, as far as she was concerned, he could do no wrong. When the time came to decide on his further education, my parents chose a small college in Przmysl; this meant that he had to travel there daily by train. After a while he changed dramatically, and began to smoke, drink and gamble. My parents knew nothing about this, but I learnt of it through friends. However, I was not the type to tell the family any secrets; the only one I told was my sister and she would not say a word to anyone.

However, in the end one of the train inspectors caught Ted and his friends smoking and gambling on the train, and reported it to my father, who also worked on the railway. There was a lot of trouble over this, as someone told the college authorities, who expelled him - Poland was a very strict society in those days, and by English standards still is.

The following term, Ted was accepted into another college in another city; Sambor, which is fifty miles East of Chyrow, and once again had to travel by train every day. My father asked the inspectors on the train to keep an eye on Ted, and he managed to finish the term, but failed the examination, so he was thrown out once more. Again, my parents had to find another college for him. My mother was always very religious, and hoped that Ted would become a priest; and at the beginning of next term my parents took him to the Niepokalanow Monastery. I felt very sorry for the monastery, who had just acquired one of the most unsuitable future priests ever. However, they were saved by the war. He entered the monastery in 1938, while we were still at Zimna Woda. He managed to stay there a whole term, and came home on vacation in 1939, and before he was due to go back, the war started, and he was involved with me in the defence of Lwow.

I am anticipating my story rather here; but I might as well finish with Ted, who was always a pest, while I am discussing him. He was taken prisoner with me, and was separated from me on the march into Russia. In fact, I never saw him again. I heard some stories from various people that he had become a gambler and an alcoholic. He wrote me a few letters, telling me he had become married and had children. However, my mother told me in her letters that his wife was a prostitute who could not read or write. In the end, he joined the Communist Party and became a director of several government owned garages, and also opened an illegal brothel and gambling casino. (Oh, yes, such places exist under Communism; they are owned by party members who can 'fix' the police!) Because Ted was such a heavy drinker he did not last long; in the late fifties his leg was amputated at the hip and eighteen months later he had a similar operation on his left leg. A year later he was dead; dying on 20th July 1962.

By that time, my mother hated him, and turned to me while I was working in England. She wanted me to come back, but my war record made the Communist bloc a dangerous place for me: but I could not tell her the real reason because of the pledges of secrecy I had made while in the army.

Let us turn to pleasanter things and more agreeable people; the rest of my family. My mother's name was Angela, and was three years older than my father. She was Polish, and I know little about her background, apart from the fact that she had one brother and one sister. My oldest relative was my Uncle Adam, and I still remember his wedding in Przemysl. He had one daughter, and she still lives in the house which he bought, and in which she was born.

My mother's sister was called Valery, and was two years younger
than her. I can only just remember her, and I do not know where she is
now, or if she is alive. She had a beautiful daughter called Irena and a
younger son called Risheck. She was married to the butcher, whose
name was Stefan, and they had a shop near Krakow.

My mother lived to be eighty-two, and (like her son Ted) lost both
her legs by amputation. She finally died in 1979; and her death was
associated with a strange incident. At five minutes to eleven on the day
of her death a shot was fired outside our house in Bournemouth. My
wife and I were watching television, and though I heard the noise, I did
not realise it was a shot. The following morning I found the bullet
embedded in the curtains, and called the police. After a few weeks,
they sorted out the mystery and informed us that some London
gangsters had been fighting each other, and had been careering
through the streets, shooting back and forth between one car and
another, and we had received a stray bullet. However, the strange
coincidence was that this shot was fired at the exact time of my
mother's death, at five minutes to eleven in Poland.

But all this was still far ahead of me in those days; I had a peaceful,
happy childhood, and I have interesting memories. One is linked to my
grandfather. He had a slaughterhouse business near Krakow, and I
often spent my summer vacation there. I used to kill the pigs and cows
and we used to drink the warm blood; actually, if you take the clots out
(my grandfather used to scoop them out with his fingers), it tastes quite
nice. I would not drink it now - the idea seems bizarre, rather horrible.
But that is later conditioning. Then, I was young, and it did not worry
me. Maybe my activities in the slaughterhouse were the reason that the
sight of bloody remains and fragments of bodies did not worry me,
later on, as much as they might have done.

My father was very tough on us children. If I did anything that he did
not like, he would just say my name, once, sharply, and that was
enough, I would stop doing whatever it was. We had to learn how to
cook, sew, wash, knit, all the domestic tasks. I did not like it then, but
I was very grateful for it later on. I can sew better than many women, or
even sew a suit. I can even extract my own teeth.

My first adventure started when I was only five: In the summer of
1929, my family sold the house where we were living and we had to
move to temporary accommodation just on the outskirts of Przemysl
until our accommodation in Chyrow was ready, and we stayed there
until February 1930. During the first few weeks of living in our

temporary accommodation, a biplane was forced to land in a nearby field; that was the first time I had seen a plane with a four bladed propellor. It stood there in the field, guarded by soldiers, and from that day on, I wanted to be a pilot.

The summer was very hot, and for some reason I wandered away from home and walked four-and-a-half miles to see my grandmother (that was my father's mother). Of course, she assumed that I had come with my father or mother, but when she found out that I had come on my own, she telephoned to my father, who came to pick me up and take me back home. I was told off, and given ice cream on condition that I promised not to do it again.

However, I had not finished wandering. During the next few days there was a lot of talk about the airplane standing out in the field; and I memorised the name of the airfield in the vicinity of Lwow. So one day, I decided to go and see my father, who was on duty at the railway. When I arrived, the ticket inspector did not stop me at the gates, for all of us children often visited our father on the station.

Once on the platform, I suddenly heard someone enquiring about the train to Lwow. The inspector pointed out the train standing on the other side of the platform. And (don't ask me how or why) I made my way to the train, boarded it and shortly afterwards I was on my way to Lwow! About half an hour later the inspector, who knew me, came along and asked if my father and mother were with me. I told him they were not, and that I was on my way to the airfield at Lwow. That was it! He locked me up with some sweets in his compartment, and later came and kept me company. Later on, I was put on a train back to the central station, my parents and a good spanking!

All in all, my upbringing was very strict. On the whole I benefited from it - but not, perhaps, where the Polish attitude to girls was concerned. Poland is very much a Roman Catholic society, and it was difficult, especially for someone who was rather shy, to mix with the opposite sex freely. This did cause me difficulties in later life.

My father expected the same obedience from our mother that he expected from us - but he did not get it. She was fiery and strong willed, and defied him. I shall always remember New Year's Eve, 1934, when she had decided to go out to a dance in the evening. My father came in, rather tired, and found himself expected to go out. He refused, and there was a row - did I say a row? - what I really should have said was, a real stand-up-knock-them-down-and-drag-them-out fight. For once, my usually calm, imperturbable father completely lost his temper and nearly strangled her. We heard something of what was happening, although we were in bed. The doctor had to be called, and she spent the next day in bed. We children did not mind - we could do what we wanted, unchecked - these adult quarrels were no concern of ours. For the following six months, my mother was subdued, and there was less of the usual conflict between my father and herself.

I began my family education in 1936, at a technical college in Lwow. My family left Chyrow, and followed me to settle in Zimna Woda, a residential village ten kilometers west of Lwow, a beautiful village, no tarmac roads, just sand, and surrounded by lovely pine trees and the occasional palm tree. Our villa was situated in a small forest, surrounded by trees. It had several bedrooms and a magnificent garden with many flowers. We also had two servants. Nearby, there was a lake. In summer, the whole family virtually lived by the lakeshore. We had a small sailing boat. Life was very beautiful and peaceful. The college was a fair distance from my home in Zimna Woda, so when I had to sit the entrance exam, I went to stay with my Aunt who lived in the city.

The examinations took four days and we had to wait a long time for the results. There were 682 applicants and only 42 places, so only the very best people would be accepted. When the local paper announced that the results would be published the next day in the college vestibule, I could hardly sleep for the tension. I was now pessimistic - but my Aunt was optimistic. The result was that when we went to look at the list, she looked at the head of the list, expecting me to have high marks, while I looked at the bottom. She found me first - I was the twenty-seventh successful candidate. I could not believe my good luck.

For the first year I went in to college every day, catching the 6.15 am train to the city, and then walking 5 kilometres to the school to save money. I passed the first year exam with reasonable marks. I was quite pleased, mainly because it was one in the eye for my brother Ted, who was not very successful at his studies, as I have already mentioned. You will also have gathered that I was not very fond of him, for which I make no apology - he was a stinker.

Of course I had many friends, and one of the best was Roman Zagurski, whom I still know - he lives in England. We met when I was ten - he was a tough boy, a real daredevil. He used to ride his bicycle on the flanges of the high girders which supported the road bridge which spanned the railway lines. These flanges were only twelve inches wide, and curved right up in the air, and he would ride there even when the trains were running below. So as not to show myself as a coward, I did so too. It was completely terrifying, riding so close to the speeding trains. One touch from the speeding monster and I would have been killed. But with the usual children's luck, I was not.

Roman and I attended the same school, and were three years together in the technical college in Lwow, though he attended only in the evenings, while I was there twelve hours a day, from eight a.m. to eight p.m. His family had less money, and evening class was all they could afford.

I was very keen on engines, and studied them at college. In vacation, I worked one month in a factory near Gdynia, where they reconditioned diesel engines for submarines. We made compression rings for the pistons, and polished them. So I learnt about diesel engines. Even now, I make my own tools: socket-spanners, ring-spanners, and ordinary spanners. I also learned a lot about ordinary car engines, and we learned in a practical way, by stripping down engines and putting them together again - it was not just theoretical. I enjoyed it a lot, because I have always been an engineer by inclination.

I also learnt about radio - by 1939 I was in the Signal Scouts, and we had our our shortwave radio station - by permission of the City of Lwow. I remember we paraded on the 3rd of May, Polish Constitution Day, with the crowds cheering us madly - Poles are very patriotic.

All this technical knowledge would be very useful to me later - indeed, it would save my life. Another ability which I acquired when young was confidence in wild country. When we lived in Chyrw, between 1930 -36, we were in the valley between the Carpathian mountains to the south, with large hills to the north. The river in the valley runs into the Dnestr, Roumania and the Black Sea. We used to collect mushrooms in the woods and there were plenty of them, big ones, in which you could easily get lost. I had to look after myself, and as a result, my sense of direction is very good, and I know things about the woods, such as that the north side of a tree is different, always from the south side, in that the moss always grows on the northern side, not the southern.

Another fact that was important in my early conditioning, and which helped me later on, was the fact that even in peacetime, Poland was a tough country. In Poland, the First World War had gone on till 1921, and there were still deserters from both sides hiding in the forests which stretched away round the town for many miles. They would ambush the roads, hold up cars, or even attack towns and villages, for there were many thousands of them. Five thousand surrendered on one occason when the Polish army held their manoeuvres. They thought that the shells falling in the forest were meant for them!

When the international trains ran through a part of Poland, they had an armoured car attached to them between Lwow and Sambor, on it's journey to Prague in Czechoslovakia, or to Budapest in Hungary, since the line ran through the forests where the deserters lurked. So dangerous were these men that we always had guns in the house - my mother had her own pearl handled pistol. It was very unlike the peaceful, civilised life of France or England today; rather a frontier feeling about it, like the Wild West.

Because of this atmosphere, when we boys went on our winter camps, we would go armed. We would have a two days' walk up a mountain to the campsite, and about a forty five minute ski run back down when we returned. Most of us carried a rifle, and at night we had to light big fires to keep the wolves and bears away. I was the school champion skier in those days, and once made a record jump of 62 metres.

It must seem strange to many people in the more peaceful Western countries to be actually worried about being attacked by wild animals. But there were plenty in the forests, and the wolves and bears used to prowl near our house in the winter. They would attack, too, because they were starving.

My father had also been in the First World War. He had been a White Russian who had settled in Poland, joining the Poles after their uprising against the Bolsheviks in 1918. He had done well, and had secured the surrender of a whole Russian division with it's officers. Later, he had been decorated by the Polish President at the anniversary of the uprising in 1932, on the hill where the Russian troops had surrendered.

I can remember him talking to my mother about his days in combat. I learned quite a lot that day - how to protect yourself, what to do on patrol - and my father told me something then which helped me a lot later. He told me never to be afraid of the whistling noise of bullets or shells. If you can hear it, it is already past you and is no longer a danger. The one that hits you, you will never hear. All in all, although I was brought up carefully, sheltered in many ways from the wilder sides of life, I was very well prepared for the ordeal which I was to endure after the whirlwind of war hit Poland in 1939.

In the meantime, I enjoyed my upbringing in Poland. It is a beautiful country, and I still miss it sometimes. It has almost everything one could wish for, and in particular the Carpathian mountains, with the Tatry peaks highest of all, where, before the war, the winter Olympics had taken place; Zakopany is the biggest city in these mountains and is surrounded by the most picturesque panoramic views. It is so wonderful one cannot describe it, only experience it in one's heart. People living there are very special; not to be compared with others. Their artistic knowledge is completely fantastic. On the west side of the Carpathian Mountains, known under the German occupation as Selesia, there are coalfields - the best coal in Europe. Further north there are many salt mines where good quality salt is produced. Eastwards, the land is rich in oil - in some places it actually oozes to the surface in people's gardens.

But while I played and learned, there was trouble brewing - and in September 1939, it came.

For several weeks before the actual outbreak of war, Roman Zagurski and I started noticing trains passing through our area, mostly military goods trains. (The Polish Army generally travelled in goods wagons specially fitted out to transport soldiers.) The soldiers were all filled with patriotic emotions, and singing songs about Poland and their love for her as the trains passed by. Many trains did not hold men, but were filled with guns and other military equipment, including horses and horsecarts. (The Army was not fully prepared for war, and much of their equipment was very out of date.) Nevertheless, the morale of the men was very high and the will to fight for freedom and democracy very strong. They must have been strengthened by the sight of so many young people, like myself and Roman, cheering them as they journeyed west towards the German frontier. I shall never forget the smiling faces of these men, many of whom never came back to their families.

In spite of this preparation, everyone (including Roman and I) thought that this dreadful war would never happen. My father often talked about the possibilities, and he thought that even if war came, the Polish Army would be able to hold the Germans back.

Chapter 2

WAR!

On the day that the war started, at 12 noon, my father and I stood on Platform No 4 of Lwow Railway Station. We were just chatting idly, domestic gossip of no importance. Platform No 4 was a platform for international trains, and the Madrid train was due. Of course, as a 'railway child' I knew all about the timetables. When I asked my father what had happened to it, he told me that he had received secret information that the train had been redirected through another country. Although war had not been declared, tension was high, and the authorities wanted to make sure the train reached Madrid, where it was ultimately bound.

Just then, I heard the noise of many aircraft engines, far away. The sky was lightly clouded over, and in the gaps between the clouds I saw many aircraft approaching the city. I was well informed when it came to aeroplanes, and told my father at once that these were foreign. My father was sure they had to be Polish. But the next thing that happened was that we saw several squadrons of Polish fighters lifting away, almost vertically, from Sknilow airfield. They began to attack the foreign planes - German bombers. The fighters did a good job, and only a few bombers reached Lwow. But for the first time, I heard bombs falling. By now, air raid sirens were moaning all over the city, people were running about, and the whole station was in a complete state of panic.

Except for my father. Very much the ex-army officer, very calm and controlled in his manner, he went to the telephone which was located at the end of the platform, and which was for his personal use. (At that time he was in charge of the arrival and departure of all the international trains on the station.) The phone was connected to Control at once, and my father's voice came over the loud speaker, telling the people to stop runnng about and to get to the air raid shelters. When the platforms were clear, he and I went to the shelters ourselves. There was panic in the shelter also. A bomb exploded nearby, and the wave of compressed air was taken by the people there for gas. My father reassured them.

When the all-clear was sounded, the passengers streamed from the shelters and boarded their trains. The Madrid train was now in, and a few minutes later my father received the signal which allowed it to depart. He was thinking out its likely route, which he thought would run through Hungary, Switzerland, Southern France to Spain and Madrid. He immediately insisted that I went home. When I arrived at Zimna Woda, a number of people approached me, very excited, gesturing and all talking at once, asking questions about the bombing of the city. I briefly replied to the effect that there had not been much damage, just a few craters here and there and a few buildings hit. When my father returned, he told us that one of those bombs had actually fallen on a block of flats owned by our family, killing several residents who had taken refuge in the basement shelter.

That evening, I and my parents discussed survival precautions, because the railway line and a railway bridge were very near our house. There was an obvious possibility that they might come under attack, and our house with them. As a result, we decided to make a bomb shelter for the house. My brother and I occupied the next few days in making it. We dug down into the soil, which was basically sand and fine gravel. When we had got down to a reasonable depth we covered the resulting hole with railway sleepers and concrete slabs and made it waterproof with a tarpaulin.

The next bomber attack came on the morning of 3rd September, and continued all day, pounding the City, the railway lines, roads and the airfield. The airfield got the worst of it. No fighters took off to oppose them this time. There were constant appeals on the radio for people to join the Home Guard and so on. News also came over the radio that a German Fifth column was active, composed mostly of Ukrainians. There had been Ukrainians living in Poland for many years. They had always hoped for a State of the Ukraine to emerge from Russia - they had attempted to form one after the Revolution. Now Hitler had offered to give them their state in return for help in his war, and they had responded. They had blown up the fuel dumps round the city, and that was the reason for the absence of fighter planes.

The bombing continued for three days; during this time the central marshalling yards to the West of the city were destroyed and became six square kilometres of bomb craters. On Sunday, as we were getting ready for Church, we heard, once again, the noise of the bomber waves, and when we looked up, we saw the Western sky black with incoming planes.

This time, however, the Polish fighters were ready for them - they took off like a string of pearls rising into the sky. Many planes were shot down on both sides,and the first wave of German bombers were completely destroyed, some of them falling within two or three kilometres of our village. Of course, we all ran off to find them, many people taking their guns with them. In actual fact, there were no survivors, but the firemen who extinguished the blaze of the burning wreckage checked to make sure there were the right number of skeletons in each fuselage!

In Church, the young priest reassured us that anyone concerned in the fighting for Christianity and freedom would not be committing a sin if they missed Mass. The next appeal for help over the radio told us that the spearhead of the German advance was only fifty kilometres west of the city. The local commanding officer issued an appeal for students with military training to volunteer to help defend the city.

As my father was an ex-army officer, and knew many young people aged fifteen to eighteen, he sent my brother and I to call on them and suggest an immediate meeting in our house. Quite a lot of them attended. Of course, I was only fifteen, and would never have been accepted in the forces if my real age had been known. But I was broadly built and looked older than my age, and my father suggested I join up with the rest.

We all walked off to join up. On our way to the city, we had to pass through open fields, and there were enough of us to make a target for the German planes. Down they came, and we had our first taste of war, as machine guns hammered at us. The bullets whistled over our heads - of course we scattered and took cover in ditches, behind hedges, wherever we could. Fortunately their aim was bad, and nobody was killed. But it was a frightening experience.

When we arrived at the city, we had to circle round it to make contact with the army on the city's northern side. Here we waited for transport to take us to the main headquarters, where we were told to report to our various colleges. At my college, I ate a hot meal and joined the Voluntary 2nd Battalion for the defence of Lwow. We changed our College military uniforms (all students wore military style uniforms in those days in Poland for everyone was a part of the defence force in the form of cadets. Dress standards were more formal then, no jeans and sweaters for us, we had to look very smart) for standard army uniform and began to receive instruction.

My first real taste of combat came that afternoon. There were four of us standing outside the college. It was three o'clock. I was with my brother and my friend Roman Zagurski and another schoolfriend, Ted Kucza. Suddenly, there were several explosions - the Germans were shelling us. Injured people cried out - bits and pieces of the church opposite fell into the street. Ted Kucza fell down. Roman and I jumped to help him. Roman took his arms and I his legs - at least I was going to, but I found that all that remained was the front of his trousers - his legs had gone. We carried him to the college basement, where there was a small temporary hospital.

After I had left him there, I leant against a wall to try and calm myself. My brother was next to me, and saw that I was distressed. He was (then and always) a heartless, cruel person, and laughed at me, saying what a coward I was. However, in war you cannot stop long to examine your own grief. Soon we were back with our new unit, and were sent by the Sergeant Major to be issued with our rifles.

And now came the comic relief. The rifles we were issued with dated from the Napoleonic war. They had long barrels and long thin bayonets and when they were placed with their butts on the ground they stood higher than a man. With the rifles came two hundred rounds of ammunition per man, and six grenades. We were rather taken aback at being issued with these ancient things, and the Sergeant Major assured us that more modern rifles would be issued to us soon.

Just before supper, we were lined up in the court in front of the college, and met our commanding officer, a full Lieutenant - Lieutenant Obuchowich. He was in his late twenties, very well built, with his face set in a cold, hard expression. He inspected us and asked a number of questions, but none of me, which, considering I had enlisted illegally, was just as well. The next day, 17th September 1939, part of our battalion was lined up in front of the college in full battledress. Lt. Obuchowich told us that the Germans were rapidly approaching the city, and we were to help hold them off. We were to be distributed among the experienced soldiers in the ratio of one among five.

Off we went, marching in two lines on each side of the street. We must have looked very young and innocent, because as we marched off, women came out of their houses, very upset to see such young people going to the front. They actually called out that we were only children and should not be allowed to go. We were typical boys of our age, however, and had very little use for female sympathy!

A little later on the Stuka bombers came over again, and we lay
down on the pavement till the raid was over. Then we resumed the
march and were nearly at the front line when we received our first
casualty. A sniper was concealed in one of the houses in the street
down which we were marching. Six of the boys at the rear of our unit
were ordered to make a search, and successfully captured the sniper.
He was a Ukrainian, one of the fifth column the Germans had planted
in our midst.

There was no question of a trial. Six of us boys were ordered to form
an execution squad by Lt. Obuchowich. The man's hands were tied
and he was blindfolded. The execution squad lined up, then it was
'Aim," and "Fire." The sniper slumped dead to the ground, and his
body was left there in the gutter.

At the front line, we were parcelled out among the regular soldiers,
and I finished up in a trench in the garden of a house. I could see a
railway embankment, beyond which there were a number of small
allotments and a road with a line of houses. Just after I arrived, a
German spotter plane came from the North, flying at about fifty
metres. We tried to shoot it down, but failed. Then it became very
quiet, and we saw no Germans; in fact there was no sign of their
presence except the artillery shells which fell in the city.

The next day, it was the same, except that we did see a German
patrol on a motorbike with sidecar, who fired at us as they moved along
the road. My brother Ted was lightly wounded in this attack and had to
be sent to hospital. I felt very lonely and wanted to cry; even more, I
wanted to run off home - I was still really very young. However, I
concealed my feelings.

Towards evening, our battalion was withdrawn from the front line to
rest at another school. Just after midnight, we were rousted out, and
marched off to the North East side of the city to guard a goods station.
We were given mortars and ammunition and additional grenades.
When we arrived at the goods station, we were surprised and delighted
to find that we were guarding thousands of loaded wagons, filled with
brand new big artillery cannon, anti-aircraft guns, machine guns,
rifles, ammunition and motorised light transport. We were really
happy to see this evidence of determined resistance by the
government, and it made us much happier in our duties.

We remained on guard there until 3am on the 23rd September, when
the Sergeant Major assembled all units at the main gate. We were told
to leave all grenades and mortars behind and march back to our

quarters, a distance of seven miles. The next day, after breakfast, we were called on parade, and told that a special announcement was to be made by a Major from the City Commmand. I think that we all must have had a premonition of bad news to come, for we all stood in complete silence, and did not gossip as we waited, as we would usually have done. We had to wait till another two volunteer battalions arrived. The battalion officers reported to the Major, and we were all told to stand at ease.

The Major made his announcement: "My beloved young soldiers, I have very unpleasant news. Our Command agreed to unconditional surrender to the Russian troops, surrender to be effective at eleven o'clock this morning."

(I should say here, since many people do not now remember it, that the Russian Red Army invaded across the Polish border on the 17th of September and met no resistance, since there were millions of Russians and only thousands of Poles - we were just outnumbered. This attack on Poland, whom Britain had sworn to aid against all enemies, was conveniently forgotten after the later alliance with Russia against Hitler!)

"This order must be obeyed. However, each individual must lend a hand to destroy as many arms as possible - ammunition will be taken care of separately. I want to advise all you young people to find civilian clothes and go home after the surrender becomes effective at eleven o'clock. The war for our beloved country is over. We have been invaded from the West by the Germans and, most surprisingly, we have been invaded by our allies, the Russians. More than five million of them crossed the Polish border since the 17th of this month. They are now at the East side of the city, awaiting our surrender.

"Our Command has no choice but to spare the lives of hundreds of thousands of soldiers, even though they would be willing to die for their country. But this is not the time. We cannot face these odds, and we are not willing at this moment, for the time is not right, to fight on a guerrilla basis like the Ukrainian Fifth Column. Life may be hard for a while, and if any can find a way, and can escape and take refuge in Czechoslovakia or Hungary, I wish them luck." He did not say goodbye, but walked out with tears in his eyes. Soon after, we heard odd shots here and there, and learned that some officers killed themselves rather than accept life under a tyranny.

We tried to make our way home, most of us in civilian clothes. But as we were walking along the streets at two o'clock in the afternoon, and were nearing the Western outskirts of the city, suddenly two Russian tanks and some Russian soldiers appeared from a side street and ordered us to halt. I and my brother could both understand Russian, but most of our friends could not. The Russian soldiers, who seemed like wild animals, were very nervous and tense. They constantly had their fingers on the trigger, and ordered us to put our hands on our heads and lie down in the road.

We obeyed, and the Russian soldiers approached each of us separately, kicking us as we were lying there to turn us around, and ordered us to empty our pockets. If they found any arms, they shot the man possessing them as he lay there.

The remainder, who possessed nothing, were allowed to get up, form three lines and told to march back into the city. Once in the city, we were ordered into the big squares, where hundreds of Russian trucks were waiting. We were ordered to board, locked up and driven away to the East side of the city to a large field. By now there were about a quarter of million Polish soldiers assembled there. We were briefly interrogated and ordered to sit on the ground. For us, it seemed, the war was over.

Chapter 3

A PRISONER OF WAR

We sat there in that field for ten days - many thousands of Polish prisoners of war, surrounded by tanks, armoured cars and Russian soldiers with sub-machine guns. We were not given food, clothing or protection from the weather. The only toilet we had was a deep hole in the ground - no toilet paper, nothing. We began to stink.

The only food we had was from Poles in the vicinity who came to the fence round the camp and threw food over the wire. Hunger was very real to us then - real and agonising. It is actually difficult for many people to realise what hunger is, for they have never experienced it. For the first few days you suffer terrible stomach cramps. After that, the pains cease, but you are constantly weak, shrinking, as if someone was squeezing you. Your concentration and powers of memory begin to suffer, and you become apathetic.

What did I feel at this time? Well, it was terrible - and difficult to describe to anyone who has not had a similar experience. I suppose that prisoners beginning a long jail sentence must feel something similar. I was broken hearted, very homesick, and felt lost in a human jungle, for the suffering was already making many people cruel and callous. All that kept me going was the feeling that what was happening was a nightmare, which could not last much longer - just because it was all so unreal. My principal wish was just to be home, near my family and a nice warm fire - for I was always cold.

At the end of the ten days, I can remember waking, huddled up against a comrade from my village to keep warm. It was dawn, and the Russian tanks and armoured cars were starting their engines. Rumours began - we were to be deported or shot, it was thought. Then someone shouted and pointed to the east. There were marching columns of prisoners of war, marching in ranks of six, not along the road but beside it. The tanks and armoured cars were in the road, and outside the lines of men who marched by the side of the road were infantrymen or cavalry with sub-machine guns.

We were ordered to get up, form lines and march. There were

protests - we heard one or two shots and saw bodies lying on the ground as we passed. The weather was bad - a mixture of snow and sleet, and by nightfall, we were extremely tired from exertion, cold and lack of food. It sounds unbelievable, but that is what happens in wartime - and especially when you were a prisoner of the Russians, for they cared very little for any rules or conventions governing the way prisoners should be treated.

Again, it is difficult to grasp the spectacle - a great line of people stretching down the road into the distance, always flanked by guards. You were not allowed to leave the line, even to perform your natural functions. You just had to squat down in the road, and people would trip over you as they pushed on.

When we were allowed to stop, we sat down and fell asleep immediately, just wherever we happened to be, without talking. We were completely exhausted. We were woken again by the sound of engines warming up, and this time we found we were to be fed - just bread, accompanied by water and tchai, which is a very weak, foul smelling Russian tea. Even so, there were fights over the meagre supplies. I was only a boy of 15, and had no chance against grown men. They just pushed me aside, and commented that I should have stayed at home and lessened their hardship by leaving more food for them.

On and on we marched. Sometimes I felt a choking in my throat - I wanted to cry but somehow could not. As time went on, however, I began to get used to the whole situation, and took everything as it came, and my emotions began to die out and disappear. I suppose I just could not afford to feel the full horror of my situation, for in fact I spent most of the war in this state.

As we marched towards the Russian frontier, I noticed the countryside change - it was obviously an area which never knew anything but poverty. Houses were built of clay only, not brick, and everything was shabby. When we reached the line of the old Polish border, and crossed the bridge into Russia proper, we noticed that though the signs were still there, the Polish guards had gone.

There was a truck standing there, loaded with raw potatoes and beetroot, which were handed out to those of us who were nearest. It does not sound very nice, but we wiped the mud off the vegetables and ate them. You would be surprised how delicious they tasted.

As we entered Russia, we encountered a number of Russians who quietly expressed sympathy and threw some food to us past our guards. I have always remembered this; the ordinary Russian did not like his harsh government any more than we did; and they did what they could even though they themselves had little to give.

As we went deeper into Russia, though, the march became harder and harder, and the situation nightmarish. The ex-soldiers around me were dying in their sleep or going half mad. They would run out of the column towards the guards and be shot after only a few steps; and it was not just a few who died this way, but thousands. The road was littered with bodies - and the fields beside the road.

March, march, march, always hungry. My own mind began to wander, and I constantly thought of food, bed and my mother. During these few weeks I hardened from being a soft home-loving boy into someone who tried to match the hard uncaring people around me. Among those grown men, I was treated like a servant, and made to do small errands - and I always got left out when food was handed around. During this period any of us who had valuable possessions such as signet rings, or wrist or pocket watches were robbed by the Russian soldiers; they would even take clothes from us if they thought we had too many.

We were just a great line of scarecrows, marching on and on, deeper into Russia. And by the end of November, we were far away from Poland, no one knew where. In the end we reached a place known as Tula, south of Moscow, and were taken to the railway station. We sat on the platforms, and a goods train drawn by two diesel engines pulled in. The men to the front of our long line were ordered onto the train. The train then pulled away, leaving the rest of us waiting. During the next few days, six or seven trains came and went, loaded with Poles. On the 17th December, I boarded a train myself. To my surprise, in front of each wagon on the train was a truck laden with food and thick, padded Russian winter clothing.

Everyone grabbed and fought for the clothing when it was issued - fights would break out over a coat or pair of trousers. We had really become like wild beasts on the march.

Along came the food. We were issued with bread, a metal drinking can and wooden cutlery. After this, we were locked in our wagons. There were sixty two people in our wagon - and no lavatory, not even a metal bin or box. There was a hole in the floor, and we had to use that. There was not even enough room for everyone to lie down, and when you did, there were no mattresses, just straw on the floor. You can imagine the conditions in this wagon - almost unimaginable in ordinary times. A filthy, crowded mass of humanity, hungry, stinking, fearful and also (paradoxically) completely bored. The smokers, of course, suffered extra agonies, and became even less human than the rest of us. All I could do was to try my best to be calm, and remember how I used to live, remember my home to reassure myself that all life was not like this.

In the end, the movement of the wagon stopped, the train came to a halt, and the big door slid open. Each person got a supply of hot water and a loaf of bread. The bread was dark brown and I estimate that it could not have been in a baking oven longer than five minutes, because when you broke it in half, inside it the pastry was not baked and tasted like clay. One could not bite it - just chew it. The train got going again. We began to form a temporary community, got to know each other. I stuck with the friends I knew from my own village, and we tried to keep some semblance of civilisation going between us, at least.

In the end, on 23rd December, we arrived on the North side of Arkhangel'sk, and were ordered to get off and get into three lines. The guards said to us: "Don't worry, there's only 22 kilometres to go!" That is about fifteen miles - a fair distance. But what they did not say was that there was no clear road. We had to march through five feet of snow.

Off we marched, a part of that great mass of people who had been herded away from Lwow. What it must have been like for the people up at the front, I cannot imagine. I was in the middle, and I walked on the snow which had been trodden flat by those before me. Even so, it seemed endless. Everything was white. Our breath froze to the edges of our clothing, and we became walking icebergs, our clothes laden with frost, icebergs trudging through deep snow.

After eight hours of this, we arrived at a camp, where we were given hot drinks and allocated a long barrack building, with great gaps in the walls, no glass in the windows - a ruin. They looked like the abandoned towns you sometimes see in Western movies. The only signs of life were nine or ten lorries, equipped, Russian style, with skis on the front wheels and tank like tracks over the back ones. However, we were out of the train at last, and it was possible to look after ourselves to some extent. There were empty oil barrels there, and some of us younger ones who had stuck together over the months began to get to work. Roman Naider and I got an oil barrel each and took it into the barracks we had been assigned. These barracks were about 500 feet long and 80 feet wide. We found some stones to put it on - there was to be no food that night, we had been told that, but we might as well be warm.

We made a fire in the barrels out of pine branches, which we broke off the trees nearby. The barracks became reasonably warm, but there was only frozen mud to lie on until someone suggested taking short lengths of thin pine branch and making them into beds. We slept around the glowing barrels, twisting and turning, first your back frozen, and then your front. Even so, for all our work, in the morning we found that about a dozen people had frozen to death where they lay.

The next day, two Russian field kitchens arrived, with the first hot food we had had for three months, and tchai, the strange Russian tea, which tastes like rum, warming, but of course non-alcoholic. The bread was like wet clay inside, but was dry on the surface. After this, we were issued with tools; lumber saws and axes. Then, as we marched out of the camp to begin work, something happened which was to change things and give me a chance of a better life. I noticed that the Russian soldiers were trying to start the engines of the trucks we had seen last night, without success.

Roman Zagurski nudged my arm, and said: "Go and help." I said: "I don't think they'll want help from me!" But he shouted to the guards: "Do you want help?" "If you can," they replied. And he replied: "I can't help, but I know someone who can." Immediately, they called to our group to halt, and a Russian asked "Who is the clever one?"

I was pushed forward. "Slavek Maslany," said the Russian, ('Slavek' is the Russian form of my name, Zdzislaw.) "Come and see what you can advise - I have drivers who don't understand engines." I walked over to the trucks and asked whether I could have the equipment I would need. He told me I could have what they had to offer, but it might not be what I really wanted. And now my technical knowledge and interests really began to work for me. I found a shallow pan, asked where the old engine oil was, filled the pan half full, put in rags and lit it. When this was put under the sump of the engine, the senior transport supervisor shouted: "Don't, there is petrol in there." I opened the bonnet and told him not to worry.

I saw that nearby there was a cranking handle, made to be used by six men, which was resting on a rack. I kept the fire going for half an hour and checked the plugs, the ignition and anything else that might be giving trouble. When the half hour was up, I sat behind the wheel and asked one man to turn it. He was amazed - and actually he did not manage it, but had to ask for help. However, after three or four turns, the engine started, and all the drivers cheered.

I then made some suggestions. All the trucks had track lines on the rear wheels and sledges on the front wheels. I said they should run one engine for ten minutes every hour right through the night. The next day, this truck could tow-start the other trucks. I also said that padded covers should be made for the engines to help to keep them warm.

I was established as the camp mechanic. A week later, I was allowed to take a truck out on the road for testing, but of course I had to have a Russian guard. We drove about together quite a lot, and got to know each other and talked freely. One day he suggested a trip to the nearest village, and the Commissar there, when we asked, gladly gave us some food and told us to come again if we needed anything. From then on, I regularly went to the village and got food for my friends; and of course my guard had a share.

Life began to improve. Just after 1940 had begun, in the New Year, I went to a Colhoz, a commune village, which operated its land and owned it as a community, and found out that sugar beet was grown there in summer. Sometimes our transport took this to the rail station. On the first day this was done, I drove one of the trucks. Some of the villagers loading the beet said that if I came back, I could take some of the beet for my friends.

I did so, and parked as near to the camp fence as possible. I called the men from my barracks, and we soon had three tons of sugar beet inside. We hoped to improve our health with the vitamins in the fresh vegetables. But of course some people looked on it as a chance to make spirit - which they did. Men who want it will find alcohol anywhere! By the end of February, we managed to fix up a hidden washtub in a corner of the barracks, so that we could wash our clothes and underwear. However, we had to do it early enough in the evening to get them dry before nightfall, because we had to wear them to protect ourselves from the cold.

I also became a rustler - I stole cows. Very simply, I would be driving along, and seen some cows unattended in a field. Then I would hop out and cut the throat of one with a long knife. (My memories of my grandfather's slaughterhouse came in useful.) Then I would attach a rope to it and manage to heave and manoeuvre the three quarter ton carcase onto the truck - or tow it behind me. When I got to camp, I would follow the same routine as with the beetroot - and the cow would vanish.

The soldier guards often helped, on the promise of a steak for themselves - they were not fed well either. They were not bad fellows.

Two, Stefan and Anton, I got on quite good terms with. Stefan was an orphan, by order of the government. When he had been young, there had been a regulation for a while that all children were taken from their mothers after one month, and put in the care of the state. He did not know where his family were. In fact, his own government had been as cruel to him as they were being to us. So he was quite ready for a little petty crime.

These food raids helped, but did not stop the regular deaths from freezing, which still occurred, even though we eventually got oil heaters, which were left on all night and watched over to ensure continuous heat. The corpses would get carried out by their friends - thus obtaining at least two days' extra rations, since someone else ate their food! We would hook our arms through the dead man's, stumble up to the food table, and draw their rations, as if they were ill and weak and could not reach out for themselves. The guards were not very interested, and did not look closely. It seems callous, but for all of us, normal human feelings had disappeared. Death just made extra supplies available, that was how we looked at it.

The cold was always with us, and made life terrible in itself. The everyday actions of life became torture. You could hardly bear to pull down your clothes to go to the toilet. When we washed our clothes and underwear, they had to be dried immediately and put on again, while we shivered by the oil heaters.

Food and the cold were the two great obsessions. Really, without first hand experience, it is difficult to imagine what it means to live in minus 60° centigrade. The top of the water well often froze completely. This meant one had to break through to get water. If you splashed some on your coat in the process, it would freeze before you could shake it off. If you touched the crank on the well shaft without gloves, the skin would come off your hands and stick to the metal. If caps were worn during the night, hair would freeze to the cap, or to the pine branches which made up our beds.

On one occasion two men were carrying a 35mm steel bar across the railway lines. One of them slipped and the bar dropped across the line and broke into three pieces, the cold had made it so brittle.

At the beginning of March, 1940, I was sent to Leningrad to pick up a generating plant and some other equipment, accompanied by the usual guard. I did well, although the journey was very difficult, and we only got to Leningrad with the help of a tractor which cleared the way in front of us through the snowdrifts. However, in Leningrad I had twenty-four hours rest, and got a couple of extra blankets, brand new Russian working clothes, and a pair of long boots.

On the journey, the guard (he was called Anton, and later became a good friend of mine) treated me more like a companion than a prisoner, and I was allowed a lot of freedom. Then, when I reached Leningrad, I decided to investigate the possibilities of escape. There was enough fuel for about a thousand miles on top of the lorry. I calculated that if I went south, I might be able to escape to the Middle East. However, I really did not know the distance. I thought Moscow to Kiev was a few hundred miles - whereas it was more like a thousand. Luckily for me, I did not try it.

I remembered seeing ships in the docks as we drove through the city. I decided to investigate and slipped away from the sleeping guard, and started walking towards Leningrad docks. However, when I got there I found that the Port was frozen. I made some enquiries, and soon realised that though I could hide on one of the ships, I would have to wait until the ice melted, and I would very likely be found. So, although I had at least two chances to get on a ship, I gave up the idea and decided to return to the quarters where I had left the guard sleeping.

After I came back, I found that the guard had been awakened and told of my escape and when I actually arrived back, the guard had already told the NKVD, the security police about my mistake. Indeed, when I arrived back they were actually questioning him. He smiled and pointed to me and told them I was the escaped prisoner.

Of course, I did not admit that I had tried to escape, but nonetheless I was taken off to be interrogated. At their headquarters, I found myself locked in a room in which there were several men awaiting some decision as to their fate. The room was extremely brightly lit, so there was no chance of going to sleep. As soon as the door closed behind me, the men there started questioning me as to why I had been brought there. It turned out that I was in the HQ of an internal espionage interrogation unit - actually, NKVD stands for Narodnyj-Komisariat Wnuternyh Diel, which is the equivalent of MI5 in this country or the CIA in the USA.

I knew by then never to discuss matters frankly with strangers, so I just gave a simple explanation. I said I was a driver in a POW camp and could not sleep, so I went for a walk. I did not offer any further comments. About two hours later, the door opened and one of the Russian officers called my name and ordered me out of the room, guiding me to an office, very simply furnished with one table and a few chairs. On the table a gun was lying.

I had been told about the gun whilst I was locked up with the other prisoners. They told me that the gun was not loaded and it was only there to provoke people into attempting to reach for it; anyone who did so was executed as a spy. After entering the room, I sat down by the table as ordered by the officer. I glanced at the gun - it was a revolver type, and anyone with experience could easily see that there were no rounds of ammunition in the chambers.

The officer sat down and wrote a few notes on some paper and then deliberately got up and started walking round the room, leaving the gun on the table. I knew that he was observing me very carefully. During the time he was walking around, he kept questioning me and accusing me directly of being a spy for either the Polish or German forces and he insisted that if I admitted the charges, my sentence would be lenient. I made no comment, just kept saying that I could not sleep and went out for a walk - and that I was only away for about twenty minutes to half an hour. This interrogation continued for about six hours, after which he suddenly gave up, smiled and told me that I would be sent back with my guard to my camp outside Arkhangel'sk.

They drove me to the quarters where my guard was awaiting me, and after telling him about my nightmare interrogation - the six hours of waiting and standing up to the endless questions had been a terrible strain, we went on to the docks to collect a foreign-made generator from the warehouse and started directly on our return journey. The guard was convinced I had really tried to escape, and he kept questioning me about it for the first few hours. However, he was still friendly, and treated me as a companion, not a prisoner. I did not trust him, however, and just insisted I had only gone for a walk. In the end, we stopped for a meal and a cup of tchai, Russian tea; when we started the journey, there was no more mention of my 'walk'. And on my return to the camp, nobody ever mentioned the incident again, and they continued to treat me as before.

The day after I returned to the camp, I heard from the Russian civilian drivers that we were all going to be sent away, and our place taken by Russians sentenced for various criminal offences. This rumour turned out to be true. I was called to the office of the Sergeant in charge of transport and he thanked me for all the help I had given with the lorries and trucks and my dependable workmanship. I was given another day off to prepare for the journey, which would commence the next day, the 19th.

The men who had been working away from the camp marched back, and I learned for the first time what a bad time they had had. They had been cutting heavy timber, big trees, to be used, in the Spring, for a new aircraft runway on the soft ground between our camp and Arkhangel'sk. Many of them were badly frostbitten. Some of them had lost parts of ears, noses - sometimes the whole of both ears. I realised how lucky I had been to be near the camp, where there was nearly always a fire.

When we were all in the barracks, I realised how many had died during that terrible winter. The barracks had been full when we arrived - now only a third of us were left. I was flung back into thoughts of my family, and I cannot describe how lonely I felt. Indeed, I constantly felt like crying and felt a choking in my throat. The only thing that made me feel better was a new friendliness in the barracks, between men who had suffered so much. The atmosphere was much improved. I parcelled out the extra food I had managed to beg or steal during my journeys in the truck - earlier, I had kept quiet about it and kept it for an emergency. In the end, I fell asleep, still thinking of my family.

The next day I forgot I was to leave, and actually went to report for work at the transport unit. However, the guard reminded me I was to leave with the rest, and I went back to the barracks. Many of the men were worried that at last they were to be shot, but somehow I was optimistic. At ten o'clock, everyone from the Camp was ordered to form in three lines for a check, and even the Commander was astonished at the numbers present - so many less than had arrived. (It may seem strange that he did not realise how many had died, but the fact was that very little check had been kept on us during the winter - the nearest village was 30 kilometres away, we were surrounded by wastes of snow, and there was literally nowhere we could go.) The Sergeant Major told him: "These are all the men who are still alive," - and the final count was taken in silence.

After that we were marched into Arkhangel'sk, to be loaded on another train, just like cattle, to be taken to where we could be useful to the Russian military machine.

Chapter 4

A GERMAN PRISONER OF WAR

When we arrived at the goods station at Arkhangel'sk, the train was already in the station. The accommodation was not quite as primitive as the train on which we had arrived, but bad enough. The wagons were filled with plenty of straw, and in each there was a kind of bottomless bucket (basically a hole which gave access to the track beneath) in a corner, which served as a toilet. In another corner there were two barrels of water, perhaps 200 litres in each, which we had to use both for drinking and washing. They allocated about 40 men to each wagon, and we were given timber to construct 4 storey high bunks on each side with a centre aisle for movement. As soon as the train started moving, we began to make these bunks.

In the centre of each wagon hung a paraffin lamp. We had been issued with rations to last seven days. Heat was provided by a cast iron brazier which stood in the centre of the wagon, which we fed with offcuts from the timber from which we made the bunks. When we went to sleep, it was dark, and we could not be sure of the direction in which we were headed. But at daybreak, after we had woken up, I looked through the narrow ventilator which was all the wagon had by way of a window, and noticed that we were passing Voznega. I remembered having seen this as we travelled from the South to Archangelsk.

After another day and a night, we stopped in the siding at Kirov. There we passed yet another night, and in the morning, without warning, the door opened and we were told to get out. We were divided into groups of 40 to 50 and told to follow the guard. We reached a heap of tools which I recognised as being railway track laying tools. I felt quite pleased, since laying track would be better than cutting wood in the heart of a freezing forest. And that was what we did - lay track to a large engineering plant where I saw (from the debris and pieces of material round the factory bay) that light tanks or armoured cars were being made.

When these tracks were completed, we were loaded once more on board the train, given a week's ration of food, the wagons were fumigated and the doors slammed again. Off we moved again, in an Easterly direction, and this time we finished up in the railway station of Sverdlovsk. A couple of days wait, and then away again, still Eastwards, among mountain peaks covered with snow and occasional high pastures with animals grazing. In the end the train stopped in the middle of nowhere. Again, we were unloaded, and ordered to break the line and replace it with railway points. We managed to do it in only about six and a half hours. While one group was doing the points, another was building the temporary track to accommodate the wagons which were waiting with a load of railway track and sleepers.

Then we were on our way once more, to be unloaded, to work, to be reloaded, fed and watered, just like so many horses. This was the way of life we led - and we were, indeed, just like so many horses. We were dragged all over the place. There was further loss of life along the way, though I was not aware of it. When we finally arrived at a camp at Aralsk, a seaside resort, the Commandant of the camp bitterly complained in my hearing that he had been promised 6,000 men and had only been delivered 4,800! The Captain of the transport tried to excuse himself, but I could not hear what was said.

At the camp, we worked at a lake where there were drying pans for salt, which we had to shovel as the heavy salt water of the Aralsk sea dried out, leaving the salt behind. Within days of our arrival, men began to die of chest and skin infections, and towards Xmas 1940 we were once again loaded on a train and driven to Kharkov to work on the railway. Then in January 1941 on to Kiev, working again on the railway, and then (in the Spring of 1941) to the small village of Tri Haty, on the River Bug, to help on the collective farm there. This work was a distinct improvement. We were not kept locked up in barracks, nor guarded, being supervised only by the local farmers with whom we lived. I was selected to drive a fourteen-ton tractor. Often we used to eat and sleep in the fields, and the company we were in was pleasant and friendly, and we often had a good time, relaxing and laughing and drinking with the local folk.

Nights of drinking generally found themselves rounded off with Russian propaganda songs. They may have been idiotic, but they were accompanied by harmonica music and they lulled us very pleasantly to sleep. However, when the harvest was ended, we were once more herded together and taken off to Podgorodnaya, where we were housed in an old school. Our first job was to erect a ten-metre high barbed wire fence round our new home, complete with a double security entrance. Inside, once more we had to erect four-tier bunks for which we had straw and one blanket as bedding. Back to tyranny! But the food remained better, because we managed to get additional supplies from the farms where we had worked.

Our next job was to work on a new airfield just by the old school where we were now confined. By the way we had to build the runway, we knew it had to handle very heavy aircraft, and sure enough, a few days later, while we were still working on the runway, the first big railway transports arrived, carrying bombs from 10 to 1000 kilos in size, to be stored about 2 kilometres East from the runway on platforms of timber to protect them from damp and corrosion. This runway was never finished, either by the Russians or the Germans.

Russia was preparing for war - and by the end of June, we heard that the German forces in Poland had invaded and were making headway very fast, the front moving forward all the time. We soon knew this news was true, for German planes began to pass by, reconnoitring overhead. And by September 1941, we knew the Germans were really overrunning Russia. German bombers came over and bombed the city 10 kilometres to the East, Piervomajsk. Russian civilians told us that in some instances, whole Russian armies had surrendered to the Germans.

One day, when driving the tractor, I passed near the railway, saw thousands of goods trucks being pulled off the track into the bare fields, something which puzzled me till several days later. We were not allowed to talk except in the old school, our dormitory. The building was infested with mice, rats and insects. During the night, mice crawled to the highest bunks and gnawed the flesh round the men's fingernails. If you failed to notice the bites, through exhaustion at the hard work, you would awake with raw flesh round your nails, sometimes on all the fingers. This was terribly painful, and later the bites would become infected and boils would develop. We tried to deter the mice in every possible way. We suspended food from the ceiling to try and keep it away from them. But the mice found a way to climb the electricity wires to the lights; from which vantage point they would jump down onto the food.

The war was getting closer. One day we heard a noise like thunder - but there were no clouds. It was the artillery, German or Russian. The discipline of the Russian army began to collapse. I noticed that some soldiers were losing discipline because of worry, others because they could not care less. No doubt the worried ones were devout

Communists, and the relaxed ones just plain ordinary people who did not much care who won. After all, what had they to lose?

We were often ordered to leave work on the runway and go to the station to unload the wagons arriving there. Often it was arms and ammunition, and sometimes the personal possessions of high-ranking Communist party members. The wagons never left - they were towed into the fields like the ones I had seen. Obviously the front was near, and the railway no longer ran further to the West. We heard that the last bridge west of Podgorodnaya had been blown up - some of us discussed the possibility of escape, but lack of knowledge of the surrounding country, and fear of the Germans, prevented us.

More and more trucks passed by on the road to the East. We were working twenty-hours a day, or very nearly, sometimes without food. Washing was unknown. No-one knew who was in command at the station. Our nerves were at breaking point - particularly those of the younger prisoners. Trust broke down, and only very close friends discussed things.

At length we were locked up in the old school, no work was done on the farms or on the runway or railway. The Russian Commandant told us to stay indoors, and we were given no food. However, there was fresh water in the taps and in the shower room. The windows were blocked up with wooden planks from the outside, and we lived by electric light. As we waited there, not knowing what was to happen, we heard heavy artillery fire in the distance.

We knew there would be fierce fighting, for the nearby town of Pervomajsk was of great importance because of the railway junction and crossroads there which gave easy access to the South to the Black Sea, East to Stalingrad, and North to Kursk and Moscow. We slept in two large halls in the old school, sixty men in one, sixty-eight in the other, and from time to time men ran from one hall to the other, exchanging gossip and information. In the distance, the German artillery got louder and louder. Tension in both rooms got tighter and tighter.

In the morning, the Russian Commandant, backed by several guards, came in and asked us all to gather round. We were told that we would be locked in for some time longer. He tried to assure us it would not be for long - and after that work would resume as usual. Some of the guards were ordered to bring food - and he warned us that if anyone was so much as seen peeping through the gaps in the boarded windows, they would be fired on. With which, he left without another word, and the guards locked us in again.

For hours we argued as to what was happening. Some believed the Commandant, while others thought he was bluffing and that the Germans had the upper hand. Around early afternoon, the airfield we had been working on was bombed for nearly two hours. When it ceased, the artillery fire was louder, drawing nearer.

We could now hear rifle shots as well, and through the gaps in the boards (we took no notice of the warning) we saw two or three Russian army trucks arriving, and the guards loading their possessions into them. One of the guards did come over, banged on the windows with a bit of wood, and warned us not to break out or make any noise. If we did, the building would be fired on. The artillery and small arms fire was deafening. Then it suddenly ceased and suddenly the whole area became very quiet, apart from the sound of engines fading into the distance.

No-one in the camp slept that night. At midnight, the lights went off, which made some of us very nervous, and then, at about three o'clock we heard the noise of traffic coming in our direction. This noise steadily increased and continued hour after hour without ceasing. The nervous tension which everyone felt drove us all out of bed. We assembled in the main hall. We talked, but in whispers - rather ridiculous, for who could have heard us? Nobody was taking any notice of us at all. There were a hundred and twenty eight of us, twenty seven of them being my friends and acquaintances from the College of Lwow (Lemburg).

Some of the older prisoners, including some who had been officers in the Polish army, formed a group to advise the less intelligent prisoners what to do. They asked all those who spoke German (about twenty of us) to step forward - and I was one of them, for I did speak German, which I had learnt in technical college, though I was not as fluent in it as I later learnt to be. Just as we had sorted this out, there was an interruption. A prisoner ran from our dormitory. He had peeped out of one of the cracks in the boards and had seen some German soldiers outside the gate.

Our informal leadership committee checked that this was true, and then decided to try and let them know that we were prisoners and did not belong to the Russian army. One of the German speakers went to a window in which the glass was missing and shouted at the top of his voice, saying that we were Russian prisoners locked up from the outside by Russian soldiers who had left during the night. The

Germans appeared confused. There were several shouts, and one suddenly removed his Schmeisser machine pistol from his shoulder and pointed it towards us, shouting: "Achtung, achtung! Look out, look out!" Whether he meant to warn his comrades of possible danger, or us, was not clear. Several of his friends followed his example, however, so it was probably us!

In the meantime, one of the committee managed to find a piece of white cloth and force it through the gap in the boarding where the glass was missing. After this, the Germans broke through the camp gates by barging them down with an armoured truck. The building was rapidly surrounded with soldiers manning heavy machine guns on tripods.

The Ober-Leutnant in charge asked the man with the improvised white flag who he was, and on being told once again who we were, and that we were unarmed, he ordered his men to unblock the door. We were ordered to come out one by one with our hands up. The German speaker who had been conducting the conversation so far went first. There we stood, surrounded by suspicious Germans with guns in their hands. There were more questions, and the German speaker was kept busy. After that, most of the Germans were ordered to stand easy, only six remaining on guard, and the Ober-Leutnant disappeared into a building used by the Russians as their headquarters.

When he emerged, he ordered a supply of food to be organised, and lists were made of our names and dates of birth. We were issued with eating utensils, and a extremely good meal was served out, with real coffee. We were then told we could keep our utensils for future use. Five of the German speakers were taken away for further questioning. They were away for two hours, and when they came back they told us that we had been a surprise to the Germans, who had not known of any prisoners-of-war in this area.

Then there were more questions for everyone: Rank held in the Polish army, area of Poland from which we originated, details of our Polish families, if any. Then another meal in the evening - very luxurious when compared to Russian rations! Earlier on, the Ober-Leutnant had told us that the local Commanding Officer would pay us a visit, and sure enough, he arrived in a big car with a motor cycle escort while we were eating. One of the soldiers shouted at us to get up from our meal, but the Commanding Officer, a Major, told us to sit down and finish eating. After the meal, we were lined up and the Major and Ober-Leutnant walked down the line, speaking to each man, after which the Major addressed us:

"Men, you have today been liberated from the Russian prison camp and we are here to give you three choices. There are some of you who either have relatives in Germany or who were actually born there. These men, five in number, will be immediately released and sent home for a holiday. For the remaining one hundred and twenty three of you, there are three choices. First, to voluntarily join the German Army and stay here to fight the Russians to bring total German victory.

"Second, we need men who are healthy and strong to join our labour units, which are called 'Organisation Tod'. These men will be free to move about as long as they work as ordered, and they will be paid for the work they do. What is more, they have the choice of sending money to their home in Poland, up to a maximum of seventy-five percent of their earnings, from which normal tax will be deducted, as with all German soldiers.

"Thirdly, you may wish to remain prisoners-of-war. If you do, this decision will be honoured. You must decide about the future by tomorrow night. In the meantime, you may move about freely and the gates will stay open at all times. However, anyone attempting to escape will be shot on sight."

After saying this, the Major went to his open car and left. Soon after, the five men who had German connections were told to get on a small truck to take them to Headquarters. These five shook hands with everyone who remained and wished them luck for the future before getting onto the truck. As they left, they began to sing a German song, which gradually faded into the distance - they were quickly adjusting to their change of side! The Ober- Leutnant smiled at this and asked us to gather round.

He told us that after we had made our decision, those joining the labour force would be issued with German work force uniforms, which followed a non-military pattern. They would also have all necessary underwear and equipment of the usual German standard. On the other hand, the men who decided to remain prisoner would be transported to Germany or Poland to the prisoner of war camps and would be treated under the Geneva convention as prisoners of war. Immediately, those who wanted coffee could help themselves from the field kitchen. The guards on the building that night would be of the same strength as around his own quarters - no more. We were warned to obey the black out rules - electricity supply was now restored, being supplied by emergency generator. He obviously wished us to feel that we were regarded with at least tentative friendliness.

We went for coffee, and then went to our bunks. Our state of mind was difficult to describe. Our circumstances had definitely changed for the better. From being helpless work animals, we were becoming men again. But as prisoners of the Germans, we had problems which the Russians had removed from us. Once again, we had choices to make!

Chapter 5

WITH ORGANISATION TOD

That first night after the Germans arrived, we were still in a mild state of shock. At first we occupied ourselves with routine chores. We managed to remove a few boards from the windows to allow us to see out, and lit a fire in the boiler so that we could have hot showers for the first time in many months. Most of us lay quietly in our bunks, trying to take in all the new events. Everyone was pre-occupied with the choice before us, and what to do next.

The next day, we were got out of our bunks by a German sergeant at 6 a.m. The field kitchen was working, and we got an excellent breakfast. Later on, about midday, forms were given out, typed in Polish and German, and a few of us were asked to distribute them to the others. Then came lunch - the flow of good food continued. We had rice soup, beef and potatoes and other vegetables and told to help ourselves to coffee. We were even asked if we wanted a second helping, and about twelve men did.

The rest of us thanked the cook sergeant, but went off to walk round the camp and then went back to our bunks to talk things over. We all came to the same decision. Joining the German army was a little too extreme - and would have been treason. But rotting as prisoners-of-war was too much to face, and would have done little good. We decided to join Organisation Tod, the labour force. After all, our labour would be only useful in the German struggle against the Russians, and none of us owed them anything!

After dinner, we had to hand in our forms, and were asked if our decisions were final. When he learned they were, we were dismissed for the night, all one-hundred-and-twenty-three of us. The following day, after the usual breakfast at six, we were lined up for inspection. After lunch we were loaded on trucks and sent off to Pervomajsk, which had been in German hands for a week, to go through hospital units for disinfection. We had our heads shaven, and were sprayed with powder to kill lice, after which we had a Turkish bath, followed by an ice cold bath, and were supplied with towels and a complete issue of clothing, from shoes to berets.

Before we had left we had been told to burn our old bunks, and on our return we set to building new ones and fumigating our old accommodation - which really needed it! The Germans certainly did everything thoroughly and properly. We really felt good - our bodies felt fresh again, and we eagerly set to work, sweeping and scrubbing the dormitory floors, windows and doors with disinfectant. We were also given another room, and some of us occupied that, so that there was more room to move about. That dinner provided us with more pleasant surprises. There was a litre of Schnapps for every five men; and everybody received twenty German cigarettes. We were told this was a weekly ration which would be handed out every Saturday night. At eight o'clock, a sergeant told us that tomorrow the place would be handed over to a labour unit, consisting of civilians of German origin, and the soldiers who had taken the camp, the Ober-Leutnant and his men, would be sent up nearer the front.

We were about to acquire new masters, and at lunch time the next day one of the Poles came in, shouting that the new people were arriving. Naturally we ran out to see what kind of people we had to work for. The truck which arrived carried only a few men, mostly in civilian clothes, though a few wore uniform, mustard coloured with a red band on the left arms with a white circle containing a black swastika. After the truck came a car, carrying a young man of about twenty-eight, and wearing civilian clothes. He was very tall, about six feet two, and very strongly built. He looked around, and went to chat to the Ober-Leutnant, who saluted him and shook his hand. They came over to us, and the Ober-Leutnant introduced him as the Commandant-in-Chief of the labour camp. After that, trucks were brought for his men, and he left. We had been handed over.

As the Ober-Leutnant and his trucks disappeared, the tall man called us to help unload his luggage and equipment. He did not formally introduce himself till after lunch, when he called us together and gave a short speech. He told us that he was Chief Engineer Terjung, responsible for the repairs and maintenance of narrow gauge railways between the camp and Vinnica. He asked for people who could help organise the camp and the work, for anyone who could work on electrical systems and repair them. He also asked for a chef and two hands to help him, for a master-blacksmith and helper, also drivers, master carpenters and trainees, and ordinary labourers.

He told us the work ahead was enormous, but possible if we all really pulled together. For important jobs we would receive a bonus in the shape of Schnapps or cigarettes or both. Then we began to be selected. Some were taken on by one German overseer, some by another. When my name was called I found myself face to face with Chief Engineer Terjung himself. I had filled my name in as a driver and an expert on car maintenance. The first job I had to do was to wash his car - not a difficult job. After that I checked water, oil and tyre pressure. I noticed that while I was at my work, Terjung watched me while he seemed to be checking the kitchen and the construction of the blacksmith's workshop. He was obviously sizing me up.

I had been given the car key, but when I tried to hand it back to him he told me to drive - he wanted to see whether I was as good as I had said I was. After all, I was only seventeen, and he may well have had his doubts.

We drove off - the area surrounding Podgorodnaya was very flat and one could see for miles - straight for the village. When we had passed it he called me to stop, and told me to get out. What a sight! To our left, as far as we could see, as far as Podgorodnaya Railway Station, there in the fields were thousands and thousands of narrow gauge railway coaches and goods wagons, standing in the fields on the bare soil.

They obviously gave Terjung food for thought, for he stood whispering to himself for a while before turning to me with a question. He pointed to several dozen narrow gauge steam engines that stood among the carriages and wagons. "Do you think that those engines are in good order? Do you have any knowledge of steam engines?" I replied, stressing the fact that my father was a station master and that as a young boy I had often had a ride on steam engines and knew quite a good deal about them. I also told him that there were some railway experts among my comrades in the labour camp.

He also asked me: "Is it true that you were studying the aero-dynamics of internal combustion engines and that you have workshop experience?" I assured him that everything I had put on my form was true. I expect he really wondered whether someone so young could have that kind of knowledge - but there you are, I had had the best opportunities and my father had seen to it that I had taken full advantage of them. As we looked around, we saw tractor marks in the ground, and I told him that the Russians had used them to tow the carriages and other rolling stock into their parking places. We needed a tractor to tow them back, but we had not got one. Terjung tested my abilities again by asking me how I would move them without a tractor's help.

I managed to come up with an idea. We could use a portable ramp with rather thick plates at the front, with two short pieces of rail welded to it. This device could be connected to the railway track proper, and the track extended towards the parked carriages. With manpower and heavy lifting jacks, the rolling stock could be manoeuvred first onto the ramp, then run onto the rails and onto the spur of track that we would run out to the 'park'. Fortunately we had plenty of men, so we should be able to put quite a lot of rolling stock back into service quickly.

Terjung was very pleased with my idea. It may have been a test, but apparently it was better than his own solution - for in fact he had none. Quite a triumph for me - or at least for my good teachers at technical school!

Back to the car we went, and drove off along the road. Here Terjung made an important find. Behind a heap of soil by the side of the road we found a fourteen-tonne Russian tractor with four smaller ones. They had soil scraping machines attached to them. The large one had a main diesel engine and a ten horsepower starting engine, which ran on petrol. I checked the oil level in both engines, the water level and also the fuel tanks. The diesel fuel tank had a missing cap, but was half full. The petrol tank, however, had the drainage plug removed and was completely empty. I was looking it over mainly for my own interest, but suddenly, behind me I heard Terjung's voice:

"Well, can we start it and make it go?" I said: "If we get some petrol and some spanners, then I can check the magneto and plugs and starter engine and we can see."

We headed for the camp and a quick lunch, and Terjung told me to say nothing of what we had found. After lunch, Terjung saw I had everything I needed, and we headed back to the tractors behind their pile of soil. I plugged the petrol tank drainage hole with a round piece of wood wrapped in cloth, poured petrol into the tank and checked it for leakage. I dismantled the carburettor, and checked to see that it was clean, removed the plugs, cleaned them, checked the sparking gap and put them back, and turned a handle to compress the cylinders.

Then, in went some petrol, I pulled out the choke, added half throttle and the engine started at the second swing. We kept the starting engine running for about fifteen minutes, as the exhaust was warming up the diesel engine's cylinder heads.

Then I climbed into the driver's seat and Terjung sat in the co-driver's seat. I then connected the clutch of the starter engine to the main gear of the main engine. After a minute, it started firing on one cylinder, then two, and then three, but the last cylinder would not fire. However, after a few minutes spent in cleaning the fuel supply pipe and the fuel injection pump the engine started again, firing on all four cylinders and we were off. We put the tractor through a few tests, and all seemed to be in order. Terjung was keen on having the smaller tractors and the soil scraping ploughs at his disposal, and I suggested towing them all behind the big tractor.

I checked the brakes on all four to make sure they were loose, hitched them up and began towing in second gear. After one false start, since all four of the small tractors were not in a straight towing line, we were ready. At the last moment, Terjung jumped off and told me to carry on, he would go ahead in his car. I got back to the camp within about ten minutes - to be met with a triumphal reception. Terjung had turned the whole camp out, telling them of my achievement. Nearly everyone in the camp was shouting and cheering my arrival, and naturally I felt very proud.

As I brought the tractors to a halt and parked them, I was surrounded by both Poles and Germans smacking me on the back and congratulating me. They knew, of course, that the tractors would save them all a lot of hard work. Terjung was standing on the top step of the camp office with his senior staff, and he shouted, telling the men that in celebration of the tractors' arrival, an extra ration of cigarettes would be given out - and I had his greatest thanks and would be given a special bottle of Schnapps for myself. When the hubbub died down, he got hold of me and invited me to dinner.

I had to answer many questions from my comrades, and also had to take a shower, so time went quickly till half-past-eight, when one of the Germans told me that Herr Engineer Terjung was waiting for me in the staff room. I found a well-laid table waiting, and was politely asked to be seated. He asked the Polish waiter to pour the Schnapps then drank a toast with me to the success of the work ahead.

It was a fantastic meal. I was still seventeen, and a good eater - and I had had very little good food during the months before the German arrival. I still remember it kindly - a large piece of steak, three choices of vegetables. But as I ate, I remembered meals taken with my family, and suddenly the full weight of the hardship I had gone through during the last twenty two months hit me full force. For so long my feelings and emotions were dead - the fact was that my life had been so terrible that I could afford to feel nothing.

But suddenly I realised that I had almost forgotten about the war. And here I was, sitting with a German, a citizen of the nation that had torn my country apart in a senseless, cruel conflict. I looked at Herr Engineer Terjung. I wondered how much he really knew about what it felt like to be a prisoner of the Russians, of the starvation, the lack of clothing, the filthy places where we slept and the thousands of miles we had to walk.

On the other hand, when I had been a Russian prisoner-of-war, I and my comrades were threatened at every step. We had been treated like beasts and work animals, and many of us had died. The Germans had treated us well, offered us pay, and now here I was sitting down to a decent meal with a man who treated me as a human being.

Terjung immediately saw I was in a whirl of emotion, and asked me what I was thinking. I told him how preferable it was to be sitting with him compared to the way the Russians had treated me. The waiter poured another drink, served us with a sweet, and I was invited to drink to a better future.

After this we went to his quarters to talk in more privacy. The waiter was dismissed, and I was told to help myself to cigarettes and Schnapps. Actually, I did not smoke - but I did not wish to say that, for fear my ration would be stopped - and I could always find a use for them as gifts or in trade with my friends, so I took an occasional puff.

I had expected discussion about the work - but to my surprise he asked me about my experiences at the hands of the Russians. I told him that was a long story, but he asked me to start anyway, and tell him what had happened since I left home. Before I had finished, he told me to go to bed and get some rest - which I did, feeling very giddy and tired, for I was not used to a lot of smoking and drinking.

The next day I had a fine hangover! But that day set the tone of my relationship with Herr Engineer Terjung. My technical ability had impressed him, and he showed himself always to be a good friend. It is typical of him that he gave me all the credit for the work on the tractors. Many men would have taken the credit themselves, to impress their staff. But that was never his way. I am happy to say that he survived the war, and is now a high official, and still my friend. I shall never divulge his identity, for although he never did anything in the war of which he needed to be ashamed, he did hold office under the Nazis. He wants to forget those days - and seeing the hell which Princess Michael of Kent went through merely because of her father's involvement in the German military machine, I cannot blame him.

That day, Herr Engineer Terjung and I started work together. We went out in the car in the same direction as before, to a place where the railway ran very near a small canyon through which ran a river. He asked me if I was familiar with survey equipment, and I told him that I was. He then told me that he had to construct a bridge to carry a branch line off the Podgorodnaya - Vinnica line across this small canyon to carry the railway to a place called Syniuha.

We worked hard all day, surveying the site for the new bridge before we went back to headquarters at Podgorodnaya. My work with my new German employers had begun, and (thanks to my technical skills once again) I had established a relationship with one of them, Herr Engineer Terjung, which was to change my whole life.

Chapter 6

LIFE UNDER THE GERMANS

I soon found out that while I was away with Engineer Terjung looking at the river we had to bridge, the Germans had been busy. They had checked out the village, and registered everyone. All the useful men had been ordered to report for work - in their usual 'correct' way the Germans offered to pay wages. I talked to the master blacksmith and explained my ideas for my portable ramp for putting the rolling stock back to work. Already, some of the steam engines had already been jacked up and lowered onto temporary rail tracks, and shunted into the maintenance shed for checking.

The next day, early in the morning, I saw the first train being pushed down the track towards Syniuha with men and equipment on board of the wagons. Two Germans and a Russian were checking the connections of the rails to see they were in order. I went out with Herr Terjung to the local village. He requisitioned the local school for our use by the simple expedient of chalking on the front door, "THIS BUILDING IS NOW OCCUPIED BY THE H.Q. OF A LABOUR CAMP." And that was that.

We then went out to the canyon to get started on the work of building the bridge. There were a lot of men there, headed by one Feldwebel Hadyk. Work began, and I was kept busy all day. Then, when I got back to the dormitory, I found a letter in my bunk from my mother! At last we were in touch again, after twenty-three months during which I had no idea whether she and the rest were alive or dead. I had sent some money to her by direct transfer, and she had written to thank me and express her enormous happiness to hear that I was alive and well. She also asked after my older brother. Of course, I did not know, since, as I have said earlier, we had become separated on the march - but naturally I wrote back, told her as much about my circumstances as security and the censor would permit, and also said that I had many old friends from my college with me in the camp, including my old friend Roman Zagurski.

Over the succeeding weeks and months we went on working hard, and at last the bridge was finished. Some of the time I was not there, but in Gajvoron four hundred kilometres away, where I was helping with the lifting and repairing of a wrecked three span bridge on the line between Vinnica and Syniucha.

This was quite an engineering feat; apart from everything else, we were still working in terrible weather conditions. The whole river which the bridge crossed was frozen solid, and much of the steel which had to be used and manoeuvred was engulfed in ice. In fact, the first thing we had to do was to chip the ice away so that we could start work. It took four days to clear one of the fallen spans of the bridge alone; and it was ten days before two spans were completely free; and even after that we still had a third span to free and the whole work of raising the fallen spans still had to be done.

We had to work in heavy overcoats and use gloves, which hampered our movements and hence the work. The cold caused all sorts of complications. The jacks we used to raise the bridge were hydraulic, and needed a constant inflow of water. To keep this water from freezing, the jacks had to be heated twenty-four hours a day with blowlamps. However, a few days before Xmas 1941 we managed to jack up the first span to the level of the railway track.

After this, it had to be rivetted into place, and this was another major headache. The old rivets had to be cut or drilled out by hand-operated ratchet drilling tools. Just one hole sometimes took two men more than a day, even with continuous drilling. There were no blow torches for the cutting of the plates, and we had to use a ten-kilogram sledge hammer and a very heavy chisel mounted on a handle. To cut a plate with these tools, a plate measuring one metre wide, and two-and-a-half centimetres thick, took five men between six and eight hours, and our hands were covered with blisters - even through our gloves.

In spite of these difficulties, the second span of the bridge was in location and secured in position at the level it was to eventually occupy on Xmas Eve. After that, the work went reasonably well - but in the middle of January we received another setback due to the cold. We were rivetting the middle span of the structure. One morning we came in to find that most of the rivet heads of the rivets secured the previous day had been sheared off. We soon found out what had happened. When the rivets had been put through the plates, they were red hot, as was the normal practice. However, the plates themselves were shrunken by the intense cold. As the rivets cooled, they started shrinking, passing some of their heat to the plates. But the plates, being large, did not absorb the heat (and thus expand) fast enough. In a few minutes, the rivets were cold, but the plates were still heating up. The plates' expansion stretched the rivets beyond their elasticity and sheared the heads off. It was quite a setback. We were able to knock some of the rivets out with sledge hammers, but the remaining ones had to be drilled out by hand ratchet, at a cost of much agonising labour.

In the end, the problem was overcome by rigging a shelter with tarpaulins round the bottom part of the span, and a fire was kept going twenty-four hours a day so that the structure was constantly heated. This ensured the problem of the rivets did not occur again, and the workers could work without heavy clothing, which speeded up the whole process. However, the smoke from the fire ensured that we came home every evening with black faces and bodies; we had to wash regularly to keep healthy; before, some of us had skimped on washing because it was uncomfortable in the cold.

This work was interrupted at one point by a terrible incident, which showed the Germans at their worst; ruthless and cruel. The trains arriving from Vinnica had to stop short of the bridge. Two a day would pull up, and the passengers would alight and cross the bridge over wooden planks which we had laid for them, and would then join the train from Syniuha on the other side, while passengers from Syniuha crossed in the opposite direction for the Vinnica train. This did not interfere with our work, because we were working inside the structure.

On one occasion, when the train from Vinnica had arrived and stopped near the bridge, there were several young Russians among the passengers. As they were walking across the bridge, one of them dropped his bag amongst the structure of the bridge, trying to make it look like an accident. However, one of the Polish labourers noticed it, and drew the young man's attention to the bag. The German group leader was standing on top of the bridge, and halted the people crossing, called to the young man, and told him to pick up his bag. The young Russian denied he had dropped anything; but the Polish labourer insisted that it was he who had dropped the bag.

The German group leader was now very suspicious, and he grabbed the young Russian's shoulder, trying to force him to pick up the bag; the young man ran away in the opposite direction, back across the bridge, not realising that there were two other Germans at the other end. They stopped him and made him go and pick up the bag. At this point, four armed sentries who were positioned about twenty yards from the bridge realised that something was wrong and started to search everybody, male and female.

During this search, the Germans found one pistol of Russian make that a girl had hidden under her skirt. She was only about fifteen or sixteen years old, well built, with blonde hair and blue eyes. Shortly afterwards another young Russian man was searched, and another gun was found on him. As this was going on, the first young man, who had run away, retrieved his bag from the bridge structure and as they were searching it they realised it contained a time bomb with a clock trigger. In a matter of seconds, there were about a hundred armed infantrymen surrounding the passengers on the bridge, and the train for Syniuha left without them. The whole lot were taken by truck to the local Commanding Officer (not Herr Terjung.). There they were held for about twenty-four hours, and interrogated, and except for the three actually found with explosives and guns, that is one girl and two men, the rest were released and allowed to travel to their destination.

The following day, we were told we were to have a day off to witness the hanging of the three Russians; and we were ordered to go to the town square of Gajvoron, where the hanging was to take place. When we arrived at the square, there were at least two to three thousand people there, hemmed in by German infantry,and the local Commanding Officer was addressing them in Russian. He told them that the purpose of making everybody in the town attend was so that they could witness how the German nation dealt with spies and traitors, and this would provide a warning for everyone, a warning never to act against German orders.

Soon after he had finished, a truck pulled into the square with the three young Russians on it, stripped naked - it was 30° C below zero. The hangings were to take place using the cross branches of the telephone poles, and the truck pulled over underneath them. They tied up one young man and the girl, and fixed nooses around their necks, but just as they turned to the third young man (the one who had actually dropped the bag with the bomb in it), he realised that he was still untied. He managed to wriggle free and jumped off the truck and ran into the crowd. The German guards, not realising what was happening, fired into the crowd indiscriminately; but he just vanished.

Then the truck with the young man and the girl in it was ordered to pull away from the telephone poles; they were left to hang. It was a terrible sight, because the noose just strangled them, for there was no drop to break their necks. They kicked and bucked and struggled endlessly before they suffocated.

Nor was that the end of it. The local Commanding Officer stood up in his open car, and started talking to the people round him, saying: "If you believe that because one man got away nobody is to be punished, you are mistaken. For every one that escapes, another two will be hung in their place." Looking around, he picked out two young men from the crowd and ordered the soldiers to take them to another truck. They were driven to the next telephone pole, and once again they were stripped completely of their clothes, their hands were tied behind their backs, the rope was put round their necks, and the truck pulled away, leaving them to hang. The Russians stood there in silence, except for the spasmodic cries of the relatives of the two men.

The local Commanding Officer once again addressed the crowd, saying that what they had seen should leave no doubt in their minds that if anyone took action against the Third Reich then they could not expect any better treatment than such as they had just witnessed. He concluded his speech by saying that in that town and that area he was the judge and the jury and his orders would be obeyed, and there would be no trial for traitors. He then walked around the crowd, which stood in silence, for nearly an hour, staring into the eyes of everyone present; a tense, eerie time, when nobody knew what he would do next. There was no sign but the sound of his boots on the stone of the square.

After this, our group was allowed to go to the cinema, which was of course controlled by the German forces; however, the film was about Poland, and it happened that the Polish national anthem was played; to my big surprise, every Pole present got up and stood to attention. The Germans could not understand this, but there was no trouble over it. After the film, some of the German soldiers asked us to go to the German forces canteen and take a drink with them. After we had had about five or six (we needed it after what we had seen), the truck came back to take us to our quarters. There, the group leader brought out the schnapps once more and gave out half a litre to every two men. The following day, work went on as usual.

All this was the more horrible because we found the Russian people as individuals very friendly towards us; some of the men even began courting local girls. But they were (not surprisingly) very cautious towards the Germans. We had as much sugar as we wanted, and made spirit out of the surplus, and sometimes got away for a meal at the home of one of the locals. However, we were basically still prisoners, in spite of the wages that we received. And although all of us under Engineer Terjung's command had a much easier time than before, and were grateful for it, we did not forget how things really were - and in my case, I never gave up hope of escape, and, as I shall mention later, did make several rather feeble and unsuccessful attempts to do just that before my real chance came.

In the end, in spite of all the difficulties, the work was finished, shortly before Easter 1942; we had the day off, with plenty to eat and drink. A last minute hitch nearly occurred when masses of ice, pressed against the bridge, ice weighed down with several hundred railway sleepers which had been piled on it. However, the local Panzer division broke up the ice with nitro glycerine and hand grenades, and our work was not lost. Chief Engineer Terjung was naturally very pleased to see the bridge finished.

With the completion of the local repairs and work, our dormitory thinned out. Many people went to Dnepropetrovsk, where more work awaited. Soon we, too, would move on. We were still being treated well by the Germans. When the bridge at Gajvoron was lifted, there was a bottle of Schnapps and 100 cigarettes, as well as a cash bonus, for everyone. And the wages were regular, and the food good. The barbed wire and high fences which the Russians had hemmed us in with were gone, and we could move about as we wished. I felt well and healthy and viewed the future with optimism.

I also met an old acquaintance: I was out driving with Herr Terjung when I saw a familiar face driving a tractor in a field near the road. I asked permission to stop, and jumped out. The noise of the tractor prevented him hearing me at first, but then he turned round. It was Anton, one of the guards who had kept an eye on us at Arkhangel'sk, and the one who had accompanied me on the journey to Leningrad when I had planned to escape: "Oh, my god," he said, "It's you. How did you get here?"

"Well, it's been a many thousand mile journey," I said. During a short conversation, he told me that after our camp moved away, the whole Russian unit who had been guarding it had been transferred South West from Moscow for action against the German forces, and the division in which he was serving had surrendered to the Germans without much fighting. He had then volunteered to join a German labour force. However, during the work he had suffered an accident, and lost two fingers on his right hand, and they sent him home. His family lived in the next village. I said goodbye, but kept in touch, and later he helped me on the tractors which I and Herr Terjung had found earlier.

About this time, I made a new acquaintance - a retired Russian train inspector called Vorlamov, who was in charge of the trains travelling between Podgorodnaya and Syniuha. Vorlamov had a very good-looking daughter, called Maria. He took a fancy to me, and very obviously was out to catch me as a son-in-law. He told me that he was strict with her, and that she had courted one or two men, but he had sent them packing - fathers had more authority in those days! To cut a long story short, he invited me to his home the next Sunday to have lunch with them. The other men in the dormitory heard about it, and started to tease me about the marriage they felt was on the horizon - and children - one, two, three or more!

My Sunday was rather spoilt, however, by an unpleasant incident. In our company, there was a lad nicknamed Carnera (his real name was Ted Kaminski) who was one of my acquaintances from college - I would not call him a friend. He was called 'Carnera' because he was outsize, with enormous shoulders, and resembled the Italian boxer Carnera who was famous in the early 1930's. I did not like him, in fact I regarded him as a big pest. As I was getting ready to go, he stood in the doorway of the dormitory, and made endless jokes, which were echoed by the other men. I ignored him - my experiences had made me very cold, composed and withdrawn. Also, I was the youngest man in the camp, and therefore expected to knuckle down to all my elders.

I started to collect my shoe-cleaning kit - and Carnera walked over and kicked the brush under the bunk. I ignored him, and started to walk towards the door. However, he stretched his arms across the doorway, and laughed at me. I politely asked him to let me pass - his response was louder laughter.

I tried to push past him - he blocked me. Then I snapped - and in those days I was very strong. I had lived through hardships that had toughened me, and the good food and work of the past few months had put me in good condition. I picked him up with one hand on his collar and the other between his legs, lifted him above my head, and threw him.

He flew through the air right across the room, and crashed into the first row of bunks - and broke them. The bunks beyond were knocked over. I must have looked terrible. When I came to my senses my hands were shaking - I cannot imagine what my face looked like. The whole dormitory became suddenly very quiet indeed.

I looked round - you could have heard the slightest noise. Everyone was dead quiet. I went out, and stood still for a while to recover my composure. I really felt very strange. That confrontation had released something in me that I never knew existed. Maybe all the frustration and anger of those long months had finally found an outlet. Certainly, I was a different man from that day onwards. From being a quiet young lad, I became very much more formidable and very difficult to push around.

I then continued on my way, rather slowly and thoughtfully. I had not realised it, but all these goings on had made me late - and my plodding pace made it worse. When I reached Vorlamov's house he was by the gate, looking out for me, and he called, "I thought you were not coming - the lunch is going to be spoiled."

At this, I came out of my trance-like state, smiled and apologised for being late, making the excuse that I had had some difficulty leaving the camp. To my relief, no questions were asked. A few minutes later I was being welcomed with vodka in traditional Russian style. Lunch was served. The house itself looked rather primitive to me, with limited space for the large family that inhabited it. The dining room was part of the cooking space, rare in those days, though familiar now, and it was also the lounge and sometimes a bedroom. In the corner of this all-purpose common room there was a very large baking oven where they cooked the dinner and baked the bread. On cold winter nights, there was a great nest of straw laid out on top of this stove where the family would all sleep together.

I gave Maria a red silk scarf with a flower design on it, which I had bought in Vinnica some weeks previously. I was asked to sit next to her, which pleased me very much, and the meal got under way with talk, smiles and laughter. It was not an elaborate meal, but was nice and tasty. I knew that food was rather short among the Russians, and suspected that they had made a very special effort on my account.

After lunch, Vorlamov brought out more drink and we listened to Russian songs on records. Some of the children sang along with the music as it was played. We began to talk about each other's home and backgrounds - but before Vorlamov talked much about himself, he sent the children outside. Only he and I, his wife and Maria remained. What he told me I have always remembered. It shows the terrible brutality of the Russian Revolution - they certainly paid a heavy price for getting rid of the Czar. This is the story he told me:

VORLAMOV'S TALE:

I had an advantage during the Revolution when it came to knowing what was going on. I had spent thirty years on the railway, and I still worked on it during and after the Revolution. Because of this, I travelled, and saw what happened over a wide area. The fact was that the Communist Party and it's Commissars were very ruthless with villages which were unfriendly to them. They used to to seal them off one by one, surrounding them with armed revolutionaries, and then burn the crops.

Then they would search the whole place for food, and when they were certain there was none left, they would leave the place to it's fate. The people slowly starved to death, and they would send in security people to check how many were still alive. Sometimes it was about twenty days before they were all dead, in some cases a shorter time. (Note: People can live for up to six weeks without food.)

When the local Commissar was satisfied that everyone was dead, a black flag was hoisted over the village, and the revolutionaries burned the houses, leaving the bodies lying inside. This did not just happen once or twice, but frequently, on a large scale in the area bounded by Vinnica, Piervomaisk, and Dnepropetrovsk. I saw what was happening. The fact was that the Communists were insecure as yet, and so completely ruthless towards anyone whom they suspected of being 'bourgeois' or a supporter of the old regime. I took my family from the village where they were living and lodged them with close relatives in Pervomajsk, where the panic was not so acute.

Then, one day, as I left my home at Podgorodnaya, I saw revolutionary soldiers gathering at the station. I knew that this was a sign for the full force of the terror to be let loose there. I was just about to finish duty, but I got on the train and travelled to Dnepropetrovsk, pretending that in fact I was just beginning a shift. Apparently some informer had told the Communists that many of the people of the village, fearing what was to happen, had left, and as a result the train was boarded by a number of soldiers, making a check. They searched the train as it was in motion. On the last carriage they had machine guns mounted, ready to shoot anyone who tried to escape.

I was reasonably safe. I was a Railway Inspector in uniform, and all I had to do was produce my papers. But I saw them checking people's hands - any man with soft hands, the sign of the upper and official classes who did not do manual work, was sent back to the last coach and ordered to jump from the train - and was machine gunned.

The women were not sent back to the last coach to die - and when they asked what had happened to their menfolk, they were merely told they were going to be investigated, and then, if they proved harmless, would be sent home. In fact, their bodies already littered the side of the railway line for many miles. I knew what was going on - I had seen similar scenes before.

After reaching my destination, I made myself very scarce for four weeks, and on my return was severely questioned. I wriggled out of it by saying that I had been visiting a sick relation. Soon after that I brought my family home. While in Pervomajsk they had been checked by the police and passed as harmless. The panic and the bloodbath were over, and they were all reasonably safe.

I then had to join the Communist Party - the alternative was to be shot. And for a long time afterwards life was very hard. The food ration was very small, and for the first five years they were lucky to get a pair of shoes each year and the only clothing available was hard work clothing - of poor quality at that. After that, things became rather more normal in some respects, but a constant air of suspicion prevailed. Everyone was encouraged to spy on everyone else, and file their reports on their friends and neighbours each week in the Commissar's offices. Sons spied on fathers and mothers - each member of the family spied on the other. If a report was not filed, or if it did not contain some report of bad behaviour, however small, then the person concerned went to a labour camp for as long as the Commissary deemed fit.

I had a better time than most, because I had occasional chances to gain some extra clothes and food through my official position - but our mental state was almost unbearable.

I welcomed the coming of the Germans - I thought they would
liberate us. I know many thousands of our soldiers
surrendered to the Germans thinking that they would be free.
Now I am not so sure.

* * *

After he had finished, he told me not to mention anything of what he
had said and of course I promised. After another drink, I left for home.
Back at the camp, I found that my status in the dormitory had
dramatically changed. No one made jokes at my expense, no one
laughed at me, and when I walked in, people tended to fall silent. I was
rather pleased about it - but I did not realise that I had done something
which was to affect me later in life. Forces had been unleashed in me
that I could not altogether control. I had become a real killer, and
much of my later wartime career had it's roots in that moment. It took
me seventeen years of nightmares after the war had ended to make me
realise that one pays a heavy price in the end for becoming like that.

A little while later I was able to help Vorlamov. It happened this
way: I was with Herr Terjung, having just arrived back from the town
outside Pervomajsk where he had been inspecting a bridge which was
being repaired, and which was standing on temporary supports only. I
was settling down to write a letter to my family when I suddenly heard
a long long whistle from the railway track, a steam whistle that lasted
three minutes. That meant trouble on the line.

We all ran to see what had happened. At the station, I found
Vorlamov in a terrible state. He was crying and saying over and over
again, "They will shoot me." In the end, I calmed him somewhat, and
he guided me to the end of the passenger wagon, and there, on the
hand rail between the wagons, there were bits of flesh - whole expanses
of the doors were covered in blood.

Vorlamov eventually managed to tell me that, while going from
Podgorodnaya to Syniuha, they came to a horseshoe bend, and he saw
headlights coming from the opposite direction. Now this bend is just
near the highway, and he dismissed the lights as belonging to a lorry on
the road, and did not tell the train driver to slow down. The next thing
was that the headlights came round the bend, just above the track, at
high speed. They were on the railway track - and hit the wagon
platform where Vorlamov was standing, at high speed.

In fact, it was a lorry, a three-tonne lorry with axles converted to
enable it to travel on railway lines. It was travelling at 80 kilometres an

hour, the train at 45 kilometres an hour, so they met at 125 kilometres an hour - an incredible impact. One of my college friends was killed in the crash, as well as two Germans from the labour camp. Vorlamov, who had basically been in charge, was in great fear of being accused of sabotage, although in fact it was a simple accident.

I did what I could to calm him down, and I went to help clear the wreckage. After I had seen everything, I reassured poor Vorlamov still further. I told him the Germans were much more reasonable and civilised than the Russians, and I felt there was nothing to worry about. It was an obvious accident. The next day, an enquiry was held, with six Germans and four Poles on the tribunal, and things went as I thought they would. Nobody, they said, was to blame. The dead were buried with as much ceremony as possible in the local cemetery, and that was the end of the matter.

My affair with Maria continued - but really, I was too naive for it to really flourish. I was completely sexually inexperienced, and though the family, who saw me as her fiance, gave me every chance with her - I was even allowed to sleep with her on top of the stove when I visited them, I never made love to her. I was rather terrified of women, to tell you the truth!

Anyway, it was only a few days after the accident when Herr Terjung told me that the camp was to be split up, and we were all going to be off in different directions as the work indicated. I was to set off on my travels again.

Chapter 7

STEALING THE TRUCK AT STALINO

On the second day after this conversation, sure enough, we were told to pack our things and be prepared for a long journey. As I packed my things, I reflect that Podogorodnaya had changed a great deal since the Germans arrived. They had erected a timber yard with vertical cutting machines, they had opened joinery and carpentry shops and also erected a small slaughter house for cows and pigs. The Poles had complete freedom of movement, and could even take two days off outside the area altogether - up to a distance of 400 kilometres, or even obtained passes to visit their family in Poland for a couple of weeks.

Our journey was not unpleasant. We were accommodated on a train with German soldiers in some of the wagons, and travelled in proper passenger carriages, and so could look out of the windows and enjoy the view. As the journey started, we were passing through open plains, but as the hours passed the scenery became more hilly. As night fell, we were issued with a snack; hot coffee, tea, or soup. There was a lot of discussion between the Poles, the Germans and some Russians who had joined the German army. The next day, we were awakened by bright sunshine. The day was quite warm, and we were now passing through a more urban industrialised countryside, with many towns. Late in the evening, we arrived at a very large goods depot, where, at a rough estimate there were 600 to 1000 lines packed with wagons carrying guns, tanks, ammunition, food and many German soldiers, some guarding the station and others in transit.

This was the Central Station of Dnepropetrovsk on the South bank of the River Dnieper. Because of some disruption on the other side of the river we had to spend the night in the waiting room, which was a temporary wooden hut about a hundred metres long and fifty metres wide. There must have been a thousand soldiers lying sleeping on the benches, tables and floor.

I got to sleep with difficulty, lying among German soldiers with rifles and guns which stuck into my back and made me uncomfortable. When I did get to sleep I had a strange dream - that the River Dnieper had burst it's banks and was flooding the station. I awoke, crying 'Flood, flood!!" Some of the soldiers awakened and burst out laughing, saying: "What flood?"

I tried to explain, and became speechless with emotion, the dream had been so real, in fact I was speechless for quite a long time. In the end, my friends managed to calm me down, and the medical staff gave me a sedative tablet. In the end I was wakened by Engineer Terjung, who said: "Why did you have to cause a panic last night?" I was really ashamed, but he just smiled and told me to find my friends and be at the platform in one hour, no later. Soon we were off again, travelling in a South Easterly direction, travelling in goods wagons again, workers and soldiers alike. It was not quite as comfortable, but the wagons had been well equipped, and we were not too uncomfortable. Also, regardless of nationality, we were all very friendly, and the Germans who had been on leave from the front line informed us that Moscow would be conquered in a few days.

Perhaps some of my readers will have been puzzled at the way I and the other Poles seem to have got on so well with the Germans, who were, after all, enemies of our country; and this point might be a good one to explain matters, which is especially difficult when talking to English or American readers who have never really experienced the harsh realities of defeat. After all, the English have not been successfully invaded for a thousand years; and the Americans not at all since their nation was created!

The fact is that many people have a very black and white view of war; they think that one always hates one's enemy, and works constantly, whether you are in the army or not, to bring about his downfall. But the real fact is that when you are actually living with enemy nationals on a day-to-day basis, you begin to treat them just as fellow human beings; which they are, and respond to them according to their natures, some good, some bad.

Also, I must emphasise once more that as far as we were concerned, we had two sets of enemies, the Germans and the Russians. And the Russians were by far the worst. For two years we had been prisoners in their country, two years of severe hardship, starvation, cold, lack of clothing, and lack of washing facilities; two years of watching our friends die for lack of basic amenities.

Then the Germans had arrived. They had behaved decently towards us, kept their promises, fed us well, given us clothing; although we had to work, we were paid and allowed to send money home to our families in Poland, money that made all the difference to our relatives, who would have suffered far more if they had not received this help. Naturally, we responded to this change of treatment; we would not have been human if we had not.

However, this did not mean that we had completely forgotten that the Germans had invaded our country. We frequently discussed the fix we were in in our dormitories among ourselves, and the general consensus was that we just had to temporarily forget about the past, co-operate with the Germans for the moment, and thus help ourselves and our families. When you come down to it, people mostly look after themselves and those close to them, however patriotic they may be.

We were, however, very well aware that the Germans could also behave badly. Indeed, the Russian prisoners-of-war were treated as callously as the Russians had treated us. The Germans gave them neither food nor clothing, made them work in dirt and frost, and degraded them till they were hardly human beings any more at all.

Indeed, so degraded had they become that the Mongols among them would even go behind the latrines their comrades used and would reclaim anything that remained undigested in the shit that was dropped there, such as dried beans, then would cook it, and eat it again. I have never even heard of such behaviour before or since.

Incidentally, another factor in our attitude towards the Germans was our general certainty that they would win; and then we would be safe from the Russians forever. And naturally, if the Germans were going to win, it made sense to be friends with them. Human beings are adaptable, you see, however patriotic they are - it's a fact of life!

After a long journey, we arrived at an even bigger goods station called Makeyevka. Our few wagons were disconnected from the train, whose cargo was anti-aircraft guns and ammunition for the most part, and we were shunted to the East side of the station. We waited there several hours until we were found by a German, now in uniform, whom we had known as a civilian at Podgorodnaya H.Q. He had had a terrible time finding us in the jungle of rails and wagons. Many of the regular soldiers who had travelled in the train had left, leaving us workers behind, and he told us to follow him for some hot food and a bed.

The next day, two trucks pulled up by the hut where we had spent the night, and took us off to our new H.Q at Mospino, a small village of about twenty buildings next to the river. The H.Q. building was on the North bank, and a great deal of construction machinery for mixing concrete, manufacturing steel girders, and so on, stood about. The occupants of the H.Q. were German, the Commanding Officer was my old acquaintance Herr Terjung, now in uniform with the rank of captain. However, his rank did not reflect his authority, which was terrific. He could even outrank the local Commanding Officer at Stalino in certain areas. I suppose this was because the Germans had realised that unless one had railways and roads in good working order, one could not do anything - especially in a country of vast distances, like Russia. Terjung was responsible for an area of country about 25 kilometres in radius, in which area he was to reconstruct and rebuild where necessary all old railway bridges, road bridges, and anything else that was required.

I became his driver once again. I was also to try and maintain all transport so that it was always ready for the use of H.Q. personnel. And it was during this period that I became a motor thief.

It happened like this: One afternoon the Chief Engineer asked me to drive him in the truck to Stalino, and during the journey, he tried to explain the job he had in mind. He told me that, once we arrived there, I was to park the truck I was driving in such a way that I was in front of a truck which he would point out to me. It would be easy to spot, since it would have American markings - it was one of the trucks sent by the Americans to Russia, and which the Germans had captured. When I had done that, I was to attach a towing chain to the American truck while Herr Terjung went to talk to the Commandant of the depot where the truck was parked.

We arrived, and I set to work in a matter of fact way to carry out Herr Terjung's orders. When I had finished, I sat behind the wheel of the new truck and waited for Herr Terjung to finish his talk. Out he came, got in the truck we had arrived in, gently edged forward to take up the slack in the tow chain, and then rapidly accelerated at full power towards the gates.

The Commandant and guards saw what was happening. They jumped on the running board to try and stop us, but I had wound up the windows, and was going, by that time, at 40 kilometres an hour. To my dismay, I heard shots being fired - later we found one or two bullets embedded in the panels of the truck. Herr Terjung had stolen the truck, and had tricked me into taking part.

I was given no time to think - he drove like a maniac in the direction of Stalino, to lay a false track, then drove North, then switched South, and then, after a headlong drive, slowed down in a narrow valley through which ran a stream and scattered bushes, pulled both trucks off the road behind a screen of undergrowth, and then stopped.

He alighted and came to speak to me, ordering me to stay in sight of the traffic on the road. I waited, and after about an hour there was the sound of a car engine, and over the rise of the small hill at the head of the valley came Herr Terjung, with two other men whom I knew. He went off in one direction, while the three of us set to and towed the American truck back to our headquarters, arriving under cover of darkness. Within seconds of our arrival the truck, an American built Studebaker with a petrol engine, had been pushed by hand into a hiding place among the Headquarters buildings. During supper afterwards, we learnt that no-one at Headquarters had ever seen a truck like this before, and we already knew that it was not in working order.

Next day, we tackled the problem. Naturally, we could hardly ask for supplies or spares from any normal source! Since I was looked on as the mechanical genius of the locality, Herr Terjung asked my advice. I checked over the truck in it's hideout, and found that the clutch housing was split. This was a problem, since there was no easy way of mending it. In the end I managed to braze the multiple seams together, grind the necessary welds, and put the truck back on the road again, and I gave it a tough test drive. Nothing went wrong.

The next day, we sprayed the truck, which was green, with sand coloured paint. We even wondered, having been ordered to use this colour, whether we were to be transferred to the African front - ? The truck was now disguised, but still a problem. As we drove it about, we were stopped from time to time and questioned about it by Special Branch police. As a result, Herr Terjung told me where there was another, similar truck, damaged beyond repair. I went there, and under the pretence of looking for other things, I removed the number plate and noted the engine number. On my return, I replaced the truck's existing number plate with the one I had taken, and put the ruined truck's engine number on the new truck's papers. Thereafter we never had any trouble, and I became the truck's regular driver, which I found very pleasant - it was a lovely vehicle.

There was one pleasant incident connected with that truck I shall always remember: We were going from Stalino to Dnepropetrovsk. We were in the truck and had picked up a huge generator. The radiator was boiling, and we were passing one or two houses near the road. As I got out of the truck for water, I thought I heard a scream, and said so to the German who was in the truck. He said it was just my imagination. We started to crank the water up, and there was a shout in Russian. I put in the crank, and said to him that we should investigate. Somebody might be injured.

I opened the door. A woman was lying on the floor, nobody about, and the baby's head was already projecting. She shouted to me for help. The German did not bother much about helping her. I asked her what she wanted. I asked what to do, and she told me to pull it gently. Then she asked me to put some hot water on the stove. By the time the water was hot, the baby was born. I did not know how to cut the cord. She had some string to tie it. The baby was already crying vigorously, and I washed it - a big boy. Eventually I cut the cord with an ordinary knife, and tied it with the string. The woman just washed herself and got up to her feet. She asked me to have a drink, and she gave us some good food.

She asked my name, and said 'Good, I'll call him Ivan - Ivanovitch.' Well, I said that was OK by me. I never passed that way again, but I hope that kid is well.

At about this time, we had a trip - we were working in Dombas (this was in August 1942), and Herr Terjung asked for volunteers for a trip to Austria; we were now regarded as railway specialists, and there was an old bridge to be reconstructed there. We set out from Stalino, and travelled through Dnepropetrovsk to Odessa; where there were bureaucratic hitches till our papers were in order to complete the journey. When we arrived, and saw the Danube, the waters were yellow, swollen with silt after a heavy rainfall, which amused us - a yellow Danube instead of the blue Danube of the song! We travelled on the south bank to the outskirts of Vienna to the goods station, which was called Prato. We then had a day off because the local command had not organised our tools and equipment.

After that hard work began; an average of fourteen hours a day for the first few weeks, and in the fourth week we were working up till midnight under floodlights. However, we did have days off, and we spent them in Prato, which has magnificent entertainment facilities; we rode on the big dipper, the ghost trains, all the fun of the fair - free, so it felt even better than usual. We would spend hours on the big wheel alone, which was then the biggest in the world. The memories of this time, so incongruous in the midst of war, remained with me for a long time after we finished the work and returned to Stalino and normal duties at the end of September.

Work continued - one big event was the construction of a stone bridge just down river from our headquarters, where Roman Zagurski was foreman of a gang of about sixty women who worked on it. Our living conditions were still good, and by and large, we were fairly content, though we naturally missed our homes and families. At the beginning of December, 1942, two weeks before Christmas, we went back on a visit to Podgorodnaya, where a skeleton staff of Germans, Poles, and Russians were producing meat at the slaughter house. And here, to my great surprise, Herr Terjung asked me if I would like to accompany him to Bavaria to his home for the Christmas holiday. I was really pleased, and accepted immediately.

He then told me that I would have to take turns at driving his car, since we would drive non-stop from Podgorodnaya, near Pervomajsk in the Ukraine, to Bavaria, a very long journey, approximately 5,000 kilometres. And we were leaving the very next day! Immediately, we prepared for the journey, and checked out the car, a French built Ford Thaunus. Herr Terjung saw to the supplies of food and water, and also loaded gifts for his family. We finished late at night and I went straight to bed. Before I did so, Herr Terjung handed me a rough map of our journey, and I went to sleep trying to memorise the names of the villages, towns and cities we would pass through.

After only a few hours sleep I was woken by a German Guard of the Labour Force, saying that Herr Terjung was ready to go. As we left, some of the Germans made jealous remarks about how lucky he was to be going home for Christmas. And off we went - it was still dark.

After we left Podogorodnaya, we travelled in a north westerly direction towards Gajvoron and Vinnica. As we were passing through Gajvoron, I could not believe my eyes, for in the town square, where I had witnessed those tragic hangings, there were six bodies hanging on the telephone poles. Herr Terjung noticed my surprise, and told me that these were not the bodies of the man and the girl who had been caught at the railway, and the other two men who had been hanged in place of the one who had escaped; he went on to say that there had been several dozen people hung there since that time. Of course, I had already half realised this, since the hangings had taken place at the beginning of the year, and we were now nearly at Christmas; the bodies would have been eaten by birds, or rotted.

About twenty miles past Gajvoron, we approached a village, and the road ran alongside the railway tracks; here more people had been executed. The telephone poles ran in a line beside the track, and they held what seemed to be an endless line of bodies, at least one to each pole, and sometimes one pole held two bodies. In a four or five mile stretch of road, there must have been at least fifty to sixty people hanging. Some of the females had had their breasts cut off. Herr Terjung made a harsh remark, which was normally unlike him, remarking that stupid people must expect such treatment, and that though he personally opposed such doings, everybody must expect to obey the law of the Third Reich. I did not understand why he said this; he was always good to his workers, and very kind to me personally. Perhaps he had noted my tendency to rebellion (as I have noted later, I made several attempts to escape while with him) and feared lest I get into trouble. Certainly it was not characteristic of him.

There was more unpleasantness to come. When we approached Nemirov, we ran into a traffic block. There were some hangings being carried out there, and everyone, regardless of rank, was being forced to go and watch. Herr Terjung tried desperately to get past (in spite of his words earlier, he did not want to witness these barbarities), but he could not get through, though naturally he was treated deferentially by the soldiers, who assured him that it would only take fifteen or twenty minutes, and then we could go. A few yards away, there was a crowd of Russians and a group of German soldiers. Each soldier had his gun ready and was standing by to cope with trouble.

We did not hear the speech of the local commander, as it had already been concluded, but we learned from another German that a few hours before we arrived, the Russian underground movement had blown up a local bridge and a German convoy which was on it at the time. As they had no idea who was responsible, they had selected fifteen people from the town and they were to hang. We had to watch, and it was as disgusting as before. After the hangings, the local commander told the people that when they discovered the final number of German casualties, they would hang two Russians for each German dead or injured. After this speech Herr Terjung ordered me back into the car, and we proceeded in the direction of Vinnica. As we neared Vinnica, we had to cross the railway lines by the station, with the city of Vinnica about a mile and a half ahead. I could not believe what I saw there. On every lamp post there was a body hanging, from the railway station right into the city itself. I lost count of how many bodies were hanging there; my mind locked itself away, not wanting to believe the truth, yet this spectacle has never faded from my mind, and even now, after all these years, I can still remember it clearly.

We stopped in Vinnica, and I was ordered by Herr Terjung to go to the department where they issued uniforms and get myself supplied with the German uniform of a Wachtmeister (Sergeant in the military police) so that I could go through the German checkpoints without any questions; I was also given the appropriate identity documents. We also refuelled the car and ate a hot meal which we had booked - yes life went on, and we ate, in spite of what we had witnessed. We were now well on our way; the journey from Podgorodnaya to Vinnica is, oddly enough, quicker in winter, when one can cross the river straight over the ice; in summer one has to use the pontoon bridge, which means a longer journey.

We started off on our way to Chmel'nickij, and arrived well past midnight. Snow began to fall, and Herr Terjung took the wheel, while I slept on the front passenger seat. I woke up at about 10 a.m. as we were about to cross the Polish border, which was marked by a small stream across which there was a bridge. Herr Terjung smiled and said to me: "Come and take over and drive back into your own country yourself." I thanked him and smiled, feeling quite cheered up by this gesture. And in late afternoon we arrived back in my own city of Lwow (Lemburg), from which I had started out three years before. I asked for permission to visit my family, who were only two and a half miles from the main road, but Herr Terjung refused, excusing himself by saying that I could visit them on the journey back. Very disappointed, I carried on driving, and when we reached Przemyl, where I had been born, we had already covered 2,600 kilometres.

Once again, Herr Terjung drove through the night. Next day we got food and drink and I checked the car, and we drove on; it was easier driving in Poland for the roads were much better than in Russia; Russian roads of those days were very bad. As we left Poland and drove through Czechoslovakia, we nearly had a serious accident. I had been driving along the winding roads in the Carpathian mountains while Herr Terjung was asleep. I was just negotiating a sharp bend, with a German truck coming up towards me and about to pass me, when he woke up. Not realising that we were on a sharp bend, he saw the car lights shining on a wall of rock and thought we were going to crash into it. He grabbed the wheel and the car skidded and spun round about four times before we crashed into a wall which bordered the road. The German truck stopped just in time. Our car was badly damaged, but not so badly as to stop us proceeding.

By late afternoon on the third day, we reached the city of Brno, where the Bren gun was invented. After that, we moved on to Vienna, which we reached at six in the early morning. We had a hot meal, and he did some shopping, clothes to give as presents to his family. Then we pressed on, down the autobahn to Salzburg; just as we passed a town called Melk, the weather and visibility were so bad that we decided we would stop; both of us were very tired and always on the point of going to sleep. We had travelled some 5,400 kilometres. At daybreak we started moving with the traffic, and reached Salzburg in the late afternoon. From Salzburg we went South, by morning we were in the Alps and had to go through several tunnels. After midnight, Terjung took the wheel again, and I fell asleep. When I woke, the car was coming to a halt outside the home of Terjung's father; a home which was large and rather grand, and which was referred to as a castle by the locals, though it did not have a moat or walls such as castles normally have.

Terjung sounded the horn several times, and out came a butler, who, seeing Terjung, called into the house, "Von Baron, Von Baron." An older gentleman came out, followed by a younger woman with children running around her. While the greetings were going on, I unloaded the car, and parked it in an open barn across the yard where there were tractors and a pick-up. Herr Terjung introduced me to the older gentleman, who was his father, and to his wife Helena and their children, two boys and a girl, and I was invited inside. Both Terjung and I were exhausted; no wonder, for we had come a long way. The butler took me to my room and told me that there was plenty of hot water for a bath, and also said that I could join them for dinner or have a meal on my own in my room. I had a bath, and came down to find Terjung playing with his youngest daughter, who was then at an age when she could hardly walk. After the meal, Terjung took me to see the local Commandant, and I was issued with a special pass which allowed me free movement in the surrounding area.

I had a very pleasant stay, and enjoyed myself, but the idea of escape was beginning to come into my head. Herr Terjung was very friendly, but he was still one of the enemies of my country. I was young and adventurous, and beginnng to become more self-confident. Somewhere in the South, in Africa, the Allies were fighting Hitler, including, though I did not know it then, many thousands of free Poles. I kept my eyes open.

I may say here that I had made several attempts to escape while I was working for Herr Terjung already - but they had not been very well thought out, and I was caught very easily. On one occasion I tried to pretend to be part of the railway staff on a train which was heading back towards Poland. But the Gestapo found that there seemed to be one too many members of staff, discovered me, and sent me back. On those occasions Herr Terjung had just told me off and left it at that, partly because he liked me and partly because I was very useful to him. But this time I intended to make a good job of it. Herr Terjung had kindly brought me right out of Russia, a journey of thousands of miles, and I was much nearer freedom now than before. I would not get another chance like this.

I noticed from my window that across the village, perhaps one kilometre away, there was a railway line. I watched and timed the trains. I also saw that the trains stopped at one point for about half an hour, and changed from steam engines to an electric engine. I wondered about the reason for the change of engine, and decided to check up. To my surprise, I found that the steam trains were coming from Berlin and heading towards Florence, Rome, and Naples in Italy. They had to change the engine because the Italian railways used mostly electricity conducted via overhead wires, not steam engines.

I also noticed that there was a customs official at the station, and came to the conclusion that this must be the last stop before the Italian border. When I went back to the mansion, I began to lay plans. As I lay on my bed, I remembered the times when I used to play between the railway carriages, and I tried to think of a place where I would be safe from customs officials and border guards. I remembered that under the passenger carriages generally used on long distance journeys there were electrical accumulators. They were fitted on each side, leaving a gap in the centre for access during maintenance. That would make a good hiding place.

I got up and moved about the house. Everyone else was asleep, and I was able to get together as many clothes as I could, taking garments which I felt were not in use and would not be noticed. I also stole some solid food which I could take to sustain me on the journey. In the end, I went to sleep just before dawn. My brain was in a whirl, and even while I had been making my preparations I could not completely tell if I was dreaming or not. I had been a prisoner, helpless, with my movements dictated by others for so long that I could hardly believe that I was taking charge of my own life again.

The next day I first collected my thoughts and convinced myself that this was no dream, and that I really was going to escape. I managed to behave normally, and went out, telling Herr Terjung that I was going to the cinema, and might be back late. This helped to ensure that any search for me would be delayed. Then I made my way slowly across the valley to the railway station where I hid myself between two workmen's sheds, and started to check up on the movement of station personnel. My new adventures had begun.

Chapter 8

ESCAPE TO ITALY

Time dragged by endlessly as I waited in my hiding place. I did not dare walk about lest I be questioned. However, I used my time to observe everything that I could about the movement of the station staff and officials. When a passenger train arrived from Italy, I noticed that none of them crossed the lines to the opposite side of the station where I was hiding. That made me sure that I had a chance to sneak on the train on my side without being noticed.

I only had a relatively short wait until I heard the whistle of a train travelling towards Italy. After it had stopped, and the changeover of the engine was in progress, I ran over to the nearest coach. Once I had found an entrance to the accumulator platform, I joyfully realised that my theory of the previous night had been correct. The two rows of accumulators on each side were securely sealed by plates on the sides of the coach and the wooden planks were secured over each at the ends of the coach to protect them from the snow and rain.

I crawled half way between the two rows of accumulators and began to wrap myself with everything I brought with me to protect myself from the frost. The temperature outside before I left the mansion was - 25°C, and I calculated that the temperature of the moving train must be lower than that, which was cold indeed. With a jerk, the train got moving. By this time, my eyes were getting used to the darkness, and I saw several gaps in the accumulator shields. I saw that the train was moving faster and faster and then we entered the tunnel and plunged into total darkness. I made myself as comfortable as possible, and actually managed to fall asleep, suffering from the mental and physical exhaustion of the last twenty four-hours.

I was woken by the sound of brakes - for a moment I did not know where I was - then I looked out through the gaps in the planks, and found we had stopped at a small station. I heard a foreign language intermingling with the German voices. The train had arrived in Italy and we were at the border station on the Italian side. After a brief stop for maintenance the train got on it's way, and I went to sleep again. I actually became too hot now, as I had so many clothes on and the temperature outside had gone up. When I woke, and took off some of my clothes, I could see the green fields outside - the snow had gone.

As I took off the clothes, I found some of the food I had taken from Herr Terjung's house. I ate - some freshly baked bread, one or two swallows of chicken, and a few swallows of water from a water canister. I felt good about being free, but very tense. I was still in enemy territory, and the responsibility of making my own decisions weighed heavily on me. I was wondering about so many things: "How shall I get clear of my hideout? What kind of people will I meet? Will I be able to communicate with them?" These and other thoughts raced and buzzed through my brain, and were only interrupted by the train's slowing down. It entered a very long tunnel, and when we emerged I could see we were entering a large town. When we stopped, I identified the station as Bologna.

After a while the train started to move again, and kept moving for about two hours. During this time, I checked out the accumulator compartment in which I had hidden, to be sure that I could get out easily at the end of the journey.

In the end, the train arrived at Florence. I crawled from one gap to another to survey the surroundings. All the passengers were getting off the train, and there was a great bustle. I lay quietly for half an hour, until the area became quiet. All I could hear was an occasional voice in Italian, as the cleaning personnel prepared the train for the next journey.

I decided to make a move, and unlatched one of the side panels and hinged it slightly out to make sure my exit would be unnoticed. Luckily for me there was no one in the vicinity, except on my far right, where I could see trains standing at the platforms with people round them. I now had the problem of getting clear of the station without running into the Italian police or German patrols. I made my way over the railway tracks and found myself in a goods yard. There were some people there, walking about and talking in very loud voices, completely uninterested in me, and I spotted the exit and walked through the cloud of noisy conversation and bustle, straight through it and out to freedom.

So, within a few minutes of arrival I found myself walking along the pavements of Florence, not knowing where I was heading. However, after a few hundred yards walk, I found myself face to face with Florence Cathedral, which seemed to me the most beautiful piece of architecture I had seen in years. As I walked across the square in front of it, I could not overcome the temptation to go in. Somehow I felt it would be a safe refuge. I suppose it was my religious upbringing coming out.

I went through the large entrance door, and the sudden darkness inside brought me to a halt. My eyes acclimatised, and steadily I began to make out the great sweep of the interior beams and columns, made out of marble and beautifully decorated at the top and bottom. At the far end one could see the light coming through the stained glass of the main dome. Slowly walking down the aisle to the front row of seats, I knelt down and began to pray. Several people entered, knelt to pray and then left. I stayed, bathed in the mysterious light that was almost like water, suspended in the quiet of the place. I had come a long way, and was very tired - and still just a boy, for all my terrible experiences.

The afternoon ended, and it was sunset. The interior of the Cathedral grew darker and darker. One of the church staff put the small lights on, and the whole of the interior glowed in semi-darkness. Suddenly I became aware that over the centre aisle from where I sat, there was a priest praying. Every now and then he looked at me, quickly, as if he did not wish to make it obvious. He and I were the only people in the building.

Soon after I noticed him, he got up and walked the length of the aisle towards the main doors. I cautiously watched his every move - I felt very alone and did not trust anyone. He locked the main door and went to the side entrance, which he checked, but left open. Then he came back along the aisle till he came to my row. He spoke to me in Italian, which I did not understand. However, I assumed that he was asking why I had stayed so late.

I knew a little Latin from college so I spoke to him in that language, saying I would like to talk to him in private. He asked me if I wished to make a confession, but I said "Not yet, maybe later." Perhaps he realised then that I wished to discuss secular rather than spiritual matters, for he quietly instructed me to watch through which door he went and to follow him in two or three minutes, but without rushing. About two minutes later, I did as he had told me, and reached the door which he had used. I could see that the room behind it was brightly lit. I knocked, and he told me to come in. It looked like the vestry where the priests dressed before mass. He asked me to sit down and closed and locked the door.

Then he sat down, with myself facing the lamp with which the room was lit. He fired three questions at once: "Who are you? Are you a priest? Are you a doctor?" He said I should not be afraid to answer truthfully, as I was among friends. This last sentence put me at ease and I felt more relaxed. I started to answer, and told him that I was Polish, and had been a prisoner of war in Russia till the Germans had liberated me. I also told him about Herr Terjung and my escape from the Bavarian mansion, my escape from Bavaria to Florence; in fact, the lot.

He politely introduced himself as a priest of the Cathedral, then asked me to sit there quietly and not to answer the door or speak to anyone till he returned. He stressed that it was impossible for him to keep me in the Cathedral and that he had to make some arrangements for my safety. He left the room and I was left on my own, wondering: "Is he going to betray me to the Fascists? Or is he going to help me?" I could hear his voice in the distance, and he seemed to be speaking to someone on the phone. I was very nervous, and I tensed myself to meet the next disaster.

The conversation ceased. Moments later, the door opened and the priest walked in with a tray full of food and a bottle of red wine. He put the tray on a small table, and asked me to move over and help myself. This gesture made me relax a little. I consumed a lot of food and drank two glasses of wine. He asked me if I felt satisfied, and began to explain what my next movements would be. He explained that he had been in touch, by phone, with a young lady who was very religious and that she would arrive shortly and take me to a secret, safe hideout. However, he did not know how long I would stay there, as arrangements had to be made for my next move, and it would take some time. He also told me that the parents of the person who was going to take me to a safe place were devoted Fascists. They must never see me.

We cross-questioned each other for about half an hour. I tried to find all the information I could about the local situation. The priest told me that the only safe place for me was with the partisans in the mountains; the partisans were not organised by one faction, but by all the anti-Fascist groups. Although it was in fact dominated by the Communist party, I did not have to join the Communists to fight with the partisans; they accepted anyone who was loyal and willing to fight for democracy. This was a relief to me - I was willing to fight for freedom, but not to become a Communist. I had had a taste of Communism in Russia, and it did not agree with me!

We were interrupted by a gentle knock on the door. It was my guide, who turned out to be a young girl with beautiful blue eyes and red hair, aged about fifteen or sixteen. I was introduced to her as Giovanni - a name which was to stick to me as long as I stayed in Italy. Her name was Shannon Berggi. She was very beautiful, but also very young, and the priest must have seen a certain doubt on my face. He told me that she was very young, but she was also a very experienced guide and dedicated both to the Church and democracy. The priest and I said: "Goodbye, hope to see you soon." (War produces these fleeting meetings all the time.) Before I left, he gave me some money and a small bag of food and wine, sufficient for the day's needs at least. He also told me that Shannon understood quite a bit of German.

We left the Cathedral through the back door, and found ourselves in a square with a number of stationary trams. She selected one and we got on. The tram moved off - it was evening, and the lights were coming on. On the tram, we began to talk, me in fluent German, she in the same language, but broken, not so easy. She told me we were heading East towards the outskirts of the city, but very little else. Most of the journey we sat in silence. She nudged me as we were coming to our destination, and told me we were going to get off at the next stop.

When we alighted, she pointed across the road to a long fence in front of a garden, saying in German: "Walk slowly to the fence and wait for me there." Then she just turned away and walked in the opposite direction. After a while I heard a voice calling me, "Giovanni, Giovanni!" and when I turned around I could see a shadow in the garden through the fence. There was a gap between a tree and the fence - I squeezed through this and found myself in a large garden. As I came nearer, the shadow turned into Shannon. She whispered: "Follow me in silence."

I followed for about a hundred yards down to the end of the garden, where we turned right between some bushes and trees, and she said: "This is it." She parted the branches of the bushes with her arms, and there was a summer house. The street lamps gave us quite a lot of light, and you could see the shadow of the big house facing the street at the other end of the garden. She took a key from her apron pocket, and opened the summerhouse door. She also gave me a small torch, since there was no electric light inside. The inside of the house consisted of one fairly large room. On the floor was a neatly made up bed, a mattress with clean linen and blankets. She told me to sit down on the mattress and make myself comfortable, and she sat down next to me. I would have begun to ask questions, but she put her finger over my lips, and started giving me instructions. She told me that she had to go back to the house, as it was getting late, but that I would be quite safe as long as I made no noise or moved about too much. She also told me that her parents went to work, and after they had left the next day, she would come and tell me everything I might want to know.

Then she got up and so did I. She said: "Ciao, see you tomorrow," and in return I took her hand and kissed it. I was so grateful to her, taking all this trouble for a stranger - and of course, she was also very beautiful. She responded by embracing me and kissing me on both cheeks. Then she left without another word. Well, I had had an eventful and tiring day, and so I got into my bed immediately and fell into a deep sleep.

I was awakened the next day by a kiss on my cheek. It was Shannon. She was extremely well dressed in casual clothes, and I could see that she had made an effort to look her best. She showed me where there was a water tap and washing facilities. The summerhouse also had a light shower cubicle if I wanted one. I had a quick wash - she sat on the mattress and watched every move. Then she went outside and brought a basket which was filled with a variety of food and a few bottles of wine. She told me to have breakfast, and said she would be able to stay with me for about three hours, after which she would try to contact people who would make arrangements for transport which would take me to a more permanent resting place. That would take between seven days and three weeks. However, she would try to come every day and bring me supplies and up to date news.

After I consumed my breakfast, Shannon called me outside the summerhouse and took me, under cover of the bushes, to a place, a few metres away where the bushes were very low Pointing to the left, she explained that the high hills in the distance were the beginning of Montegiove, and beyond were the mountains of the same name. There were the hidden headquarters of the Toscana partisans. Then she pointed over to the right. "You will go there," she said, "In those mountains, in the Pratomagno area, between Montegiove to Arezzo, there are well over 15,000 partians of all nationalities. Well, that is all I can tell you about that."

When we got back to the summerhouse she told me she was going to teach me to speak and write Italian as much as she could. Without further ado, she produced a German/Italian dictionary and a writing pad from her basket. She asked me to read the dictionary and write down the words I read. As I did so, she corrected my Italian pronunciation. My first lesson lasted two hours, and she told me to practise the words she had taught me as much as I could, since they were the keywords, the basis, of the Italian language.

Having unloaded the rest of the food and wine she had brought, she kissed me again on both cheeks, and left me, telling me that she would not see me the next day, but would come the day after. She also asked if I had a watch, and when I said I had not, she told me she would get me one. Then she vanished into the bushes, making for the house.

While she was away, I was very much on my own in the summerhouse, with nothing to do but look at the bushes. So I made up my mind to really apply myself to learning the language and practising the words she had taught me. With all the time I had to fill up, and with the help of my memory, which has always been very good, I made a lot of progress. And when Shannon came back, two days later, I astonished her by greeting her in Italian and starting a conversation. Her beautiful blue eyes snapped wide open, and she was very pleased and surprised.

After that, we spent a lot of time learning and teaching Italian. However, other things developed between us during the two weeks I spent in the summer house. On some evenings, when she could get away, she just came to spend time with me, and love began to build between us. The kisses on the cheek became kisses on the mouth, which I returned very willingly. By the end of the second week we were making love.

It seems incredible, looking back at it, those embraces in the dark summerhouse among the bushes, with her parents sitting up in the big house which I never entered, and enemies all around me. It was an oasis of affection in the midst of war - but a limited one. Two days after the end of the second week, she wore a sad expression on her face as she came to see me. In a short while, she said, a man would come to take me to the mountains.

Tears came to her eyes as she told me she loved me. I loved her too, and we both felt completely unhappy at the prospect of parting, having found each other in this completely unexpected and dramatic way. But time was short, and we had no space to properly express our feelings. She kissed me passionately once more, and then turned and walked out. Minutes later, she came back with a stocky man with a face that showed signs of open air living. He was introduced as Captain Zio of the partisans. Shannon told me to go with him and do as he asked me.

Zio went on ahead, and left us to embrace once again. Shannon gave me a last kiss and whispered: "I will never forget you, and I hope that when the dreadful war is over we will meet again." Then she led me out of the gardens by a back way, through a gap in the fence and several other gardens, and then told me we had to stop and wait for Zio to bring his vehicle. She kept saying: "I hope to see you again - I know you will be back."

A moment later, we heard the sound of a motorcycle engine and Zio came into sight, driving a three-wheeler pick-up. I jumped into the cabin with him (it was a vehicle very much like the little three wheeler cars of today) and off we went towards the main road from Florence to Arezzo. Another stage of my adventures was about to begin.

Chapter 9

WITH THE PARTISANS

As we started our journey, Zio said to me I must pretend to be dumb if we were stopped, but informed me that there were no German guards on the road and that we should have a peaceful journey. It was about twenty or thirty kilometres on the main road, but, if necessary, we could take the country lanes leading to the foot of the mountains. We passed the town of Pontasieve, and then the main road started to climb. He pointed out features of the landscape as we went. To our right was the River Arno. "This," Zio told me, "Goes right down to Florence and this is the main barrier the Germans have to cross to get to us, because there is only one place where they can cross by road and rail, and that is a few miles ahead."

Half an hour later, we stopped on top of a hill and he showed me: "Here on the left is the railway bridge and the road bridge, which runs over the River Incisa. Down below is the River Arno, which is joined here by the Incisa. It is very deep here. See, the railway bridge goes into a tunnel. This is five kilometres long. The railway goes through the tunnel to Florence to the right, and to the left it goes to Arezzo." After that we set off again, down the left hand branch of the road, going down now, till he showed me a town to the right. "This is our major source of food - Figline Valdarno." He also told me there was a powerful radio station in the town which passed the partisans' messages to the Allies and elsewhere. To the left, at the top of the hill, there was a very beautiful villa with a winding road leading up to it, lined with tall pine trees. He told me this was the Villa Monichoro, and that the landlord there supplied most of their wine (Italians consider this a necessity of life) and also organised doctors and medical supplies.

Soon after this, we passed through another village, and reached the main road at the foot of the mountains. Zio told me that if we had been heavily loaded we would have needed a tow, the slope was so steep. The road was very beautiful, being bordered by many tall trees of various kinds, and would have made a really scenic drive in more leisured times. We travelled up it for about five kilometres before we stopped and drew off the road into a spacious yard. There were many partisans here. To the right there was a large building, half stone and half timber, in front of which Zio parked the pick-up. We were soon surrounded by curious people, all talking loudly. Zio shouted to them:

"I have brought you uno Polako, a Pole, who has come to join us - you'll get to know him later when he has seen the Commandant." Taking my left arm, he pulled me upstairs. When we entered, I could hardly see anything, having been outside in the bright sunshine. I was left in a room while Zio went to see the Commandant. I heard loud conversation, and a few minutes later I heard: "Giovanni!"

In the room I entered, there was a large, rather crudely made table against the far wall. Around it were a few chairs and a number of people, sitting and standing. There were no uniforms, everyone was in civilian clothes. A man behind the table got up and politely asked me to step forward and shake hands, which I did. He asked me if I wanted anything to drink, and when I accepted, he picked up a carafe of red wine and handed it to me.

In spite of all this consideration, I felt that I was in for an interrogation, and I was right. The man I was speaking to was a deserter from the Italian army, a Colonel - the other men with him also had held various ranks. They asked me endless questions, in both Italian and German, and this went on all afternoon. In the end, they asked me to go outside and wait for Zio. While I waited, many different partisans came and tried to talk to me, but in spite of Shannon's teaching, my Italian was still poor, and though I could understand many words, I could not yet carry on a conversation.

In the end, Zio came out of the building, and said: "Very well, you are in, and first of all you must spend two or three days getting to know the lie of the land up here." He also pointed out a big barn, which he said was the communal dormitory - though most men preferred to sleep in the open. At this point, he asked me (I had been asked before) whether I was sure I did not wish to join the Communist party. I said "No," once again, and he shook hands and assured me, "It doesn't matter."

He started to question me about my knowledge of rifles, submachine guns, artillery, anti-aircraft guns, grenades and explosive. Knowledge of these things was essential to a partisan. It was also important to make friends in the neighbourhood. He warned me that I should not trust anyone and should tell nobody of the way I had reached the mountains. The only person with whom I could discuss these matters was my Commanding Officer. My first patrol would involve me joining a backup party.He told me that I was to keep in the background. The object was always to ambush German convoys if possible. The convoys always moved at night to avoid the Allied fighters and bombers, but this gave the partisans their chance. He told me that I was only to set foot on the road or take part in the fighting if it was absolutely necessary. Otherwise I was to stay back in the woods in reserve.

He also said that we were supposed, officially, to take Germans as prisoners, but because of shortage of space to imprison them, and men to guard them, we were to ignore this. He said:

"You must leave the road after an ambush ensuring that every enemy is dead, and all equipment one hundred per cent destroyed." He then looked me in the eyes and asked: "You're not afraid, are you?"

I answered: "After all these months of war, and after what I have learned in the Russian Prisoner of War Camp, and then in the German Forced Labour Camp, I don't think anything could ever frighten me again. I have seen whole graves full of bodies that are no longer recognisable as human beings."

He tapped me on the shoulder and said: "That is good, that is very good, I only wish we had more men like you, we would then have no trouble with young men running away every night. Don't let that happen if you are in charge here, you may as well kill them if they run away. If the Germans catch them, they will, before killing them, torture them and extract all the information about us that they can. And remember, nobody but the Colonel knows how many men we have, not just here but in other places too. Every few kilometres among the mountains we have a band like this - and of course 99% of them are trustworthy. But there is always the 1% who are not. So do not discuss anything with them - do not tell them of your past or mention any other bands of partisans to them." He also warned me that we had to practise self-sufficiency here in the mountains - our guns, ammunition, and clothes had to come from the Germans, though the local people did help us with food.

The next two days I spent walking around the locality, getting to know the place. And on the night of the second day, I went out with my new unit for the first time. We were in two groups, the attack group and the back-up group. The attack group consisted of about fourteen to sixteen men, led by a man called Omar, and a similar number under Zio forming the back-up group. We started off with the attack group in the lead, both units walking in single file, a few yards apart so that each man could see the man in front.

We walked down the mountain for about three and a half hours, after which we were suddenly ordered to stop. In the semi-darkness we could see the road running from right to left, with a very sharp bend. We could hear movements as the attack group planted traps and set them in position. Then we waited, in complete silence. Time has no meaning in these circumstances, as we crouched in the darkness, just waiting for the Germans to come past. You are surrounded by blackness - even the small sound of your body shifting position seems magnified. A cough is an explosion. You are bored - yet tense.

We waited in this state till about 10 pm or ll pm, when the convoy arrived. First a tank, then a small armoured car leading a convoy of six trucks under canvas, with another armoured car bringing up the rear. As soon as they appeared around the bend, the silence erupted into endless explosions and gunfire. Machine guns were firing and grenades were exploding in a continuous roar.

Nor did it just last a few minutes - it went on for nearly an hour, the firing growing less as the resistance lessened. Then it ceased, and everything became quiet with the exception of the noise of the fire as it consumed the burning trucks, and the occasional explosion of a fuel tank. Also there was the occasional shot as the partisans shot any Germans who were still alive. As I said, the official policy was a lot of nonsense and we took no notice of it. The only Germans we ever took alive were people who could be useful to us.

Then we retreated - the attack group going first - the back-up group second. To my surprise, on the homeward march nothing was said. Hardly a word was exchanged during the whole long walk up the mountain. I had not seen any of the fighting, being back in the woods, and I wanted to ask questions - but nobody said anything at all.

About six o'clock in the morning, with the sun shining, we reached Headquarters on the mountain. Most of the men from the attack group went in to the H.Q. building for a short while, and the rest fell down on the straw which was heaped around the barn and immediately fell asleep. Some of the men who were ill, and who had stayed behind, convalescing, came round with blankets to cover the sleepers and keep off the early morning dew.

The next day I was allocated to the attack group that Omar

commanded. I learned that he, Omar, had been a Lieutenant in the Italian infantry. On our way down the mountain (we went down practically every night) he talked to me constantly, trying to teach me what I needed to know. He told me to stay close to him with my short barrelled Italian rifle and six grenades. When the battle was drawing to a close, I was to grab hold of as many guns and ammunition as I could from the Germans. Whatever the size or calibre, I was to take it, as it could always be exchanged with another group if we did not want to keep it. I was also told to find more suitable arms for myself.

We did not go in the same direction as the previous night, but after climbing and descending a small mountain we sought out another bend in the road. As I was part of the attack group this time, I had to sit behind Omar in the rocks to protect him and follow his instructions during battle.

When a convoy came along, the fighting started, an incredible roar of explosions and gunfire just like the last time. In the light of the explosions, you could see the Germans running to and fro. Some tried to run away, but if they ran into the woods on the other side of the road, the other half of our group was waiting for them, and they would die there.

A number of them tried to surrender to us, but any who did so were just shot immediately where they stood, shot in the front, shot in the back, in spite of their pleas for mercy. There was no chivalry or heroism here. Every partisan was fighting for his life and for the people in the surrounding countryside who supplied and fed us, and the Germans were too much hated for anyone to want to spare them anything. After all, they shot all the partisans they could catch. They had sowed the wind, and inherited the whirlwind, as the saying goes.

They fought hard for their lives, too, and the battle went on for several hours. As it was coming to an end, I was given an order by Omar to start collecting arms, and to check the trucks before setting them on fire. I picked up six Schmeisser machine pistols, twelve Lugers and a large quantity of grenades, and dragged them a few yards up the hill. Later, working by the light of the burning trucks, we collected everything that was of use and carried it about a kilometre up the mountain. Then we went to the cache where we had left the remaining ammunition and guns and carried them up the hill too. We had to repeat this three times before all the loot was hidden safely enough to be left. Other carriers would be sent out from HQ for it later.

By the time I arrived back, my legs could hardly carry me, I was so tired. Now I fully understood why men fell into a deep sleep after dropping on the straw. However, I could now count myself a real partisan. I remembered the Germans who had tried to surrender, only to be shot down without mercy. It had been a brutal bastard business - but then, it was a bastard war and I was now a fully paid up member.

Chapter 10

A BASTARD WAR

So that was my introduction to life in the partisans. I was six months fighting with them, and every night was an ambush of shadows that suddenly exploded into the flames of combat.

On virtually every night we would go out to ambush the Germans - only occasionally would we have a rest period of some thirty-six hours. We would leave at sunset and arrive on the road in darkness. The Germans did not start to move till midnight. The first essential of an ambush was a lookout to give warning. He would be placed a kilometre down the road, while we would be hidden by a bend, where the lorries had to slow down. He would signal us with a torch, and we would be ready to spring the trap. If there was a Panzer armoured car at the front or back, we would attack them first. They would be travelling at 30 miles an hour, but when they rounded a bend, their speed would drop to about 15 to 20 miles an hour. That would give us our chance. We wore rubber soled shoes, so as to make as little noise as possible against the steel sides of the armoured vehicles. With that to help us, we would jump onto the top and drop a grenade through the trap on the top.

As I said, we would jump at the bend, when the car (or light tank, whichever it happened to be) was travelling slowly. An advantage was that there used to be a big gap between the Panzer and the next vehicle, and the driver there would not know there was anything going on until the car exploded. And then the road was blocked, and the driver and all those behind him were trapped. We destroyed the last vehicle as well, so as to block the road - generally, it was another Panzer.

Our men were generally 15 metres apart. There were about 14 men in my platoon, which was commanded by Omar, whom I have already described. I soon got on good terms with him, and every night as we went down the mountain I would discuss the plans for the coming night with him. I was helpful to him, and he taught me a lot. About a month or six weeks later, I took over command of the group from him, when his hand was blown off by a grenade. He had to leave the mountain, but survived the war.

So now I was in command, and had to make the decisions. It may seem strange, my being put in command when I was so young, younger than many of the men I commanded. I was still not yet twenty, after all. But the fact was that Zio, who made these decisions, had quickly come to see that I was a potential group leader. I was better educated than many of the others, and I had been through a great deal which had hardened me far beyond my years. Also, many of the Italian partisans had homes nearby, and were always liable to desert and go home when they were tired of the fighting. I had no such temptation.

Shakespeare said: "Uneasy lies the head that wears the crown," and he was right. Being leader means a lot of work and worry, and often very small thanks. I got little sleep, because I had to go down to the road constantly to plan my next ambush site. I never used the same place twice. Some people would use my places a few weeks or days after I did, but I always insisted on using somewhere completely new.

I was always careful in what I did - I have always been a perfectionist in everything. I was fussy about my weapons. I always carried a Schmeisser machine pistol which I always carried on ambushes - and I was very choosy about my grenades. Always English or American - it was amazing how many people were killed with their own grenades. The German grenades - they had wooden throwing handles - were not very good. Sometimes the wooden handle would break and pull the firing pin - and then you only had four seconds to get rid of it. Also there was the danger of an accidental explosion letting the Germans know what you were doing.

The Schmeisser machine pistol was one of the most successful small arms made during the World War II period, by the way. They were accurate, durable, and reliable, and we stole them from the Germans whenever we could.

When I took over the platoon, I was tough with my men and tolerated no indiscipline. This meant that sometimes I had to be very hard, and sometimes had to take a gun out and threaten a man who was disobeying orders - especially when they panicked in a tight corner and tried to run away. I used to say "If you run, you will certainly die. If you fight the Germans, you have a chance to live."

Because of this, my men never ran away, and what is more, I only lost one man in six months, at a time when whole platoons of partisans were wiped out. A lot of men deserted from the partisans, and went home because they could not stand it. You had an average of one new face a week. This happened to my platoon too, but not as often, and once I got known, I had many volunteers to replace those I lost. The fact was, the more sensible ones knew that with me, they had a better chance of survival. There was one French lieutenant, who was as strict as I, and he, too, had many volunteers, more than he needed.

We were a mixed lot in the various camps around the mountains. But the two main factions were the Communists and the Democrats. I joined the partisans who were the democratic partisans, and they never robbed the people. But the communist partisans would rob everything of value that they could find in a village. All the food came from the villages. They would leave the food on the road and we would leave the money in the same place. The Communists would just commandeer everything they wanted, even from the poor. We would rob only known Fascist sympathisers.

Mind you, many partisans took rings, ornaments and so on from the dead Germans - but I never bothered. Partly because I was so far from home - the others could hide the stuff in their homes - but also because I did not bother with money while in the war. Money made people more ready to kill you, and there are a lot of people around who held life cheap - especially in my part of the war. So, when we had a haul from a German convoy, I would keep very little for myself. When we captured a German lorry, we could not always drive all the way to headquarters. The road was so awkward, and with so many bends, bends so abrupt and narrow that often you had to reverse six or so times to get round them. So I used to take the lorry to the nearest village, and told the villagers to help themselves, and to keep the lorry if they wished. They would either strip the lorry down, or take it back to the main road, away from their homes, and burned it.

In my part of Italy, I am called 'Golden Giovanni' because I took nothing except ammunition, clothes, a nice Luger - a .62 with a six inch barrel, things that I needed for my work. This was not true of everyone. One of the lesser known facts about war, especially irregular wars and odd corners of war such as mine, is that many of the participants make a lot of money out of it.

The Communists and we others got on all right, since we were fighting a common enemy we had to tolerate each other - but we never discussed politics. Actually, I have made this a life long rule, never to discuss politics or religion except with people I know well. Otherwise, all you get is quarrels and bad feeling. In any case, in those days, I had so little sleep, I had little time for abstract chitchat - I only got three hours of sleep, as I said. I could not do it now, but in those days I was tough, and could take it, and could outlast everyone else.

There was certainly a lot of work to do. For instance, every morning, you had to clear bodies off the road from the previous night's ambush. There was a big drop to the river - they had to be dragged over the edge and dropped for the animals to eat. I did the cleaning by myself.

One of the problems of writing about those days is that we frequently went through experiences which, if you experienced them in civilian life, you would have talked about for months. But to us, they were commonplace.

For example: One Sunday I was down in the valley. Once in three weeks we went down the mountain and were put up for a night with a family down there. We had some good food, slept in a clean bed, rested, and were treated like princes by the families whose war we were fighting. It was about 10 am in the morning. I was sitting on the verandah, just in my underpants, cleaning my Schmeisser, when a 20 mm cannon opened up on me, bang, bang, bang.

The shells went just over my head and embedded themselves in the wall. I had to move quickly. I just pulled on my boots and grabbed the nearest gun - our guns were lying all over the place, and my own was in bits. There were a few of the round magazines which fitted sub-machine guns hanging on a belt, and I grabbed that too, jumped off the verandah, about a five foot drop, ran down the garden, jumped over the first hedge, ran across another garden, jumped a another hedge, another garden, another hedge, then I fell and fell and fell, and hit the ground 60 feet below. I fell with legs wide astride, and so hard that my chin made a dent in the freshly dug garden soil beside my shoes. Looking back, I cannot see how I survived it.

After that, I made haste to look for the Germans and attack them. The other partisans in the neighbouring houses came out and joined the fight. The battle lasted for one and a half hours, and in the end the Germans turned tail and ran.

There was a notice on top of our mountain, setting out the name and height of the mountain, and the distances to various local places. Allied planes, attacking the local railway, had to pull out of their dive very sharply to avoid the mountain. These pilots were all young, and very jokey, and on the way up, they used to machinegun the sign, which was virtually shot to pieces after a week.

I remember this in connection with one of the attempts which the Germans made to destroy us. We did not usually attack on a Sunday, preferring to rest. However, the Germans had no such inhibitions.

One Sunday, they attacked, and captured a young Italian sentry. He must have given them information, for the Germans located us. We had no warning; all of a sudden hundreds of sub machineguns opened up on us, late one night, as we relaxed round HQ. We escaped as usual up the mountain, scattering in all directions.

These were the best tactics, for the man who is higher up a slope has an advantage over someone who has to climb from below. This time the Germans tried to catch us out - they dropped parachutists all around that sign at the top of the mountain. We were caught in a crossfire between the men attacking up the hill, and the paratroopers fighting downhill from the sign.

Well, that was cunning of them - but we still had one advantage: we knew every stone, every tree, and they did not. So we lay low and kept quiet - all we could see of them was the occasional flare of their weapons as they fired. They advanced, and advanced - if it had been daylight, we would have seen their faces. Suddenly, they started worrying, I think, and stopped firing. They waited. They stayed where they were - and waited for daylight.

But as soon as the sun came up, we could see them, and they were soon running, even the paratroopers ran, right through our lines downhill. Every stone concealed a man of ours. Our knowledge of the terrain took a terrible toll. Many Germans ran over a 500 foot drop which we knew and they did not. There were many bodies at the foot of the cliff before the fight was over. Goodness knows how many men they lost. But afterwards, we picked up and salvaged for our use two truckloads of weapons, heavy cannons, 20mm and 30mm, machine guns, sub-machineguns, grenades, the lot.

They never came back again as long as we were there. The young sentry was never seen again. Maybe he betrayed us willingly, who knows? So many people turned traitor. Some people had to openly collaborate with the Germans - that was OK as long as they let us know. But a traitor - his house was burnt and he was shot.

The partisans had rather a grim sense of humour. I remember once a couple of Germans were caught making an attack on our headquarters - again, on a Sunday. When they were brought back to Headquarters, a fight developed. I think one of the Germans did not like being pushed by the partisan guards. And a fist fight developed, which ended in the Germans being stripped.

The partisans lined up in a double line, and the two naked Germans had to run between the human alley thus made - which terminated in a dense patch of scrub, bushes with sharp branches - nearly impenetrable.

What they did not know was that the scrub ended abruptly in a 600 foot drop. Just as one of the Germans went over, one of the partisans shot him, and he fell down, down, and got caught in the fork of a tree which stuck out of the cliff. He stayed there for about a fortnight - nobody bothered. Such events were commonplace - there must have been 1,000 bodies at the foot of that cliff, men and women of all nationalities who had been found out as traitors and made to run over the cliff to their deaths.

Mind you, life in the mountains was not always dangerous and hectic. In fact, as a rule, when we were not under attack or down the mountain in ambush, life was very peaceful. It was hard work going down the mountain and marching back again, about three or four hours of hard walking each way, not to speak of the work and the fighting we did while we were down there.

So when we were at home we made ourselves as comfortable as we could. Outside our headquarters there was a very large barn, about five hundred feet long and about one hundred feet broad; before the war bales of straw and animal food was kept. However, while we occupied the premises it became a dormitory for all the partisans, with straw spread out all over the floor. No individual had a permanent bed space, we just all huddled down together; especially during bad weather, and the weather was bad when I arrived. This was in the third week of January 1943, and there was snow on the peaks of the mountains.

This did not worry me a lot. I had come from the Russian winter, and to me the Italian mountain temperature was just like early summer. But most Italians never experience real cold, and they were amazed that I did not wear an overcoat and regularly showered in the waterfall nearby that ran down the mountainside and cascaded into the stream.

We led a very simple life; the battle-weary men coming back from the road after an attack never bothered to have any meals; just a glass of wine and they would drop into the straw and fall asleep. That was in the winter. In spring and summer, we slept outdoors in the open air. We just slept as long as we felt necessary, and the open air kitchen had constant hot food available twenty-four hours a day. It was manned by Italian women who had volunteered to help the partisans; generally they came up the mountains for a week at a time and then returned to their families.

I expect you have already noticed that I always talk about the food - well, I make no apologies for that. Food is very important in wartime, because you are often not sure of getting it. And I have always liked food anyway, and like to eat well. The food on the mountain was typically Italian; mostly spaghetti, ravioli, cheese and prosciutto coscia (matured ham) and bread, which was baked daily in a field baking oven. There was wine too, red or white, dry or sweet, also cognac and many men used regularly to have a quarter pint of it before going to sleep.

The group leaders could not be quite as self-indulgent as the rank and file, as I quickly found out. We sometimes never slept at all for about two or three days because of urgent intelligence investigations, and three and four hours sleep was the norm, except for those periods of rest I have already mentioned, when we were the guests of the farmers or other people who had homes near the mountain. Apart from intelligence and fighting, they had to file reports every morning on returning to base. We generally left each day at about six or seven o'clock in the evening, and returned between five and eight in the early morning.

Time ceased to exist; except perhaps for some of the Italians who lived locally and regularly visited their families and friends. For the rest of us, we lived in a limbo. Every night you went down the mountain, not knowing if you would come up again in the morning. Nobody could even plan with certainty for a week ahead; and the future, what would happen next year or after the war, was completely irrelevant. It was ridiculous even to think about it.

Our organisation was simple. Each unit of the partisans was commanded either by an officer who had deserted from the regular Italian forces (for of course they were Hitler's official allies), or people who had proved their worth as leaders. All the units came under the partisan local headquarters in the various areas; each local headquarters commanded many groups. In my particular area the headquarters was Monte Giove, which in turn came under the control of Toscana in Florence, where they had access to a local radio transmitter and the longer range radio station which sent messages to the allied forces in Britain or to Cairo, in Egypt. The citizens of Florence were especially loyal to the partisan cause and to each other; only devoted Fascists or common criminals would betray them - the latter for money. Many of these criminals were double agents, who would sell information about the Germans to us, but they were never allowed up the mountains; they would be met at some rendezvous and dealt with and paid off. The fact was that they did not care for anyone, and could not be trusted; the ultimate capitalists, out for Number One all the time.

I have said our headquarters were at Monte Giove, and so they were for most of the time I was there. But when I arrived, they were elsewhere. However, there came a time when the Germans were very active in the mountains - this was before the episode of the parachutists - and we had to shift and trek to new headquarters on Monte Giove. And this was one of the episodes which very nearly went the Germans' way. It could easily have turned into a complete and utter disaster.

To move headquarters, we had to march thirty miles in one night with our arms, boxes of ammunition, mortars, the lot. Well, it was very tough. Men and boys were falling down, dead beat with exhaustion, one after another. I was in the rear, and I had to be very tough sometimes to make them get up and keep moving - and pick up their burdens too, for we could not afford to lose them. My knowledge of the people I was dealing with was essential. I could tell which one was faking and which was genuinely exhausted. I carried a huge load myself - I was very strong in those days.

Our aim was to reach the top of a hill. Along here ran the road from Forli to Pontasieve. If we could cross it in darkness, we would be safe. But it was daylight when we reached the road. The German convoys stopped moving in daylight because of the American air force and the R.A.F., so the road itself was empty. Zio's men crossed the road first, and a few minutes later the rest of us got across. It was about nine o'clock in the morning, and the sun was high on the horizon when my turn came to cross the road, and I was the very last.

From the road, the ground descended into a small valley where there were a few dozen trees and among them the partisans were already dotted about, lying on the ground. We were just worn out. Literally, we just dropped down on the grass, dotted here and there, and went to sleep.

Unfortunately, the Germans were not as sleepy as we were. There were German bunkers overlooking us, of which we did not know. They spotted us, which was hardly difficult. The only precautions we had taken against being spotted were not to actually go to sleep on the road itself. We paid the price. In the middle of the afternoon, about three o'clock, we were awakened:

BANG BANG BANG - mortar shells falling - not on our position, but near enough! My God, what confusion! Several hundred partisans leapt up and some started running. Luckily, Zio was there, and he started firing over our men's heads. I also stood with my gun ready and shouted: " The only way you can run is towards the Germans." It was the only way to steady them and bring them under discipline once more.

They took up their weapons, and they started off, after collecting all the ammunition boxes. Only one thing saved us, and that was that the Germans could not see precisely where we were, and just guessed at our position. Thus the mortar shells fell quite a few yards away, and we suffered no casualties. In the end, the Germans carried on shelling the empty position we left, and we managed to get clear of them, and nobody was hurt. That was quite largely due to Zio and myself. If they had just run off blindly, some of them would have been killed, for sure.

By midnight we came to a deep valley near Monte Giove. There were three or four houses there, and we asked for food. The first, she would not give us anything. We asked the neighbours, and they confirmed she was Fascist. Her hands were tied, all food was taken, some given to the neighbours, and her house was burnt.

We came to a bridge, with one German sentry at the end, and another one walking back and forth across the bridge. We had to cross it, it was the only way over the river - men carrying great loads of ammunition and heavy guns cannot swim. I was told: "You speak German, go and talk to them." We did not want to kill them, because the shots would have made a lot of noise, and there might have been other Germans in the neighbourhood.

I walked quietly along the road, and said: "Entschuldigen, enschuldigen, mein camarade." He turned, "Halt, was wollen sie? What do you want?"

I said: "Slow down, slow down, I would like to have a word with you." I had my Schmeisser behind me. He was about 43 or so. I went on: "Look here, take yourself a walk for ten minutes."

He said: "Why? I have a friend here."

I said: "Tell him the same thing. If he wants to live, just let him be blind. Go away, you don't see anything. It would be good for his health."

When he asked me why, I told him there were eight hundred men with me who wished to cross the bridge. He asked me who they were, and I told them it was none of his business! And he just looked at me. "Jawohl," he said, lit a cigarette, and started walking away. And that was that! He saved himself and his friend, and we were saved a fight. I waved to Zio, and the column started moving across the river. Then we just had to walk across, over one big hill and across the valley and we were on Monte Giove, our new headquarters.

That was when the Americans starting bombing bridges in Incisa. The river ran in a semicircle round the hill - two railway tunnels went through it. In one month, the river ran the other side of the hill. The hill had moved! It is incredible what heavy bombing can do. The Germans would put up a bridge, and the Americans would bomb it the next day. One lot would bomb the bridges, the others the anti-aircraft guns. The pilots and crews, if shot down, always got away - the Italians looked out for them everywhere. There were 200 guns round the bridge, and they shot down 500 super fortresses in 2 months. What waste and destruction - but that is typical of war.

As I say, so many things happened. They were not always unpleasant. And to follow the next story, you must understand that one gap in my technical knowledge was motorbikes. I had never learned to ride one. My only experience of them consisted of going round the garage at home on an old Triumph with a big square brass tank and a leather belt drive.

I was in the mountains as usual, when, one day a typist came to HQ riding a Maas motorbike; 1100 cc it was, a huge machine. Well, I was young and stupid, and I wanted to try it, even though I could not ride it. So when he asked me if I had ridden a motorbike, and I said, "Oh yes."

To begin with, I couldn't find the gear - I had never driven with a pedal gear. It stalled. Third or fourth time, I got it into third gear and went downhill, going far too fast. Soon I was at the bottom of the mountains, and I saw a girl by the side of the road, hitchhiking. She knew I was with the partisans - I was quite well known among them, and she said: "I have a letter, it's very urgent, it has got to go to HQ." She meant our headquarters in Florence.

I don't know what came across my mind - she was a good looker. And without thinking, and in spite of the fact it was a drive of about 40 kilometres, I drove her there and dropped her outside the cathedral in Florence. After she had delivered the letter, she wanted to come back with me. I had to cross the river, and we ran into trouble. As we were breezing along, I saw an SS roadblock ahead, placed in the form of a zigzag, so everyone had to slow down.

There was no question of stopping. I had no papers, and could have got into a lot of trouble - firing squad trouble. I slowed into second gear, and saw that everyone at the roadblock had a Schmeisser. I thought: "Schmeissers or no Schmeissers, I am not stopping here." I told her to hold on. I put on the throttle, and I went through that roadblock like a whirlwind, driving on one wheel - not by design, but by luck. Somebody touched me momentarily, the bullets were whistling round us. Then I slowed so as to get the front wheel down on the road again.

I accelerated as much as I could to get away from the roadblock, and streaked along. I did well, but when I reached the mountains and slowed down, she had disappeared. Whether she had jumped or fallen off, I did not know, I was so occupied with the machine.

However, the mystery was solved in the end, for I met her in Cairo. She worked for British Intelligence. We had a good laugh about it.I asked her what she was doing there, and why she had slipped off the bike, (for it turned out she had not fallen off). She said: "Oh, Giovanni, I was afraid you were going to betray me." She was not going to HQ but to a partisan short wave radio station in Florence, to make contact with the British Intelligence.

Well, I did not hold it against her - but looking back, I shudder at my foolhardiness. Once again, I could easily have been killed.

Chapter 11

THE VILLA MANICHORO

As time went on, we got bolder, and made attacks on the Germans further and further from the mountains. While we were on one of these raids, we had information from an Italian girl about a villa called the Villa Manichoro, where there were over a hundred Polish and Russian men of the German labour force, and only about ten to fifteen Germans, some in uniform, some in civilian clothes. The Italian girl said some of them expressed a wish to join the partisans. Because I was a group leader, and spoke Polish, Russian and German, I was chosen to lead the attack on the villa.

From the intelligence on the previous day, there were no other forces in the vicinity. There were 15 of us, and I was walking first. We went off course, and finished in front of the villa, and not behind. Instead of being at the top of the hill, we were half way down. We had a beautiful view down the zigzag road, and we found the telephone line, and cut it. But it was difficult - we only had bayonets and knives, and it sparked when we cut it. What we did not realise, by sparking it, it rang, and soon after, two Germans on a motorcycle came down the road, and we realised they were looking for the broken cable.

We went straightaway to the East side of the villa, where there were high hedges, and a little dip, four or five feet deep. We lay in the dip, and I lay by the shed they were using as a field kitchen, waiting for the first recognisable person. Someone came, and of course it was too dark to make out their features, but I said "Hande hoch - hands up," my gun at the ready. When he turned round, it was Roman, Roman Zagurski, my old schoolfriend who had been in Russia with me - I could not believe it. He said: "Don't shoot," and I said: "I am not going to kill you, don't be daft."

He then said: "There is a Panzer division here - they moved in last night." I asked where. He said: "There are tanks all round - in the next villa, and two thousand Germans soldiers here."

I said: "Do you want to escape?" We talked for a while, and in the end, Roman suggested that he bring out Roman Naider, the most

educated of our crew, and he would chat to me through the hedge. So
that was done, though I was afraid - I was worried that we might have
been overheard. But Roman Naider came out, and said: "Zdzichu..."
That was my name. "Yes," I replied...

"We have no chance to escape, but let us know where we can contact
you." I told him next night he was to go down the road - he would find
a girl waiting - whoever wanted to escape should follow her and we
would meet them. We then retreated, south into the valley between
the Villa Manichoro and the next villa. As we approached the next
villa, we were walking up the hill on which it stood. We were spread
out across a wheat field in a line, pushing it aside as we walked. It grew
much higher than it does in England - right up to your chest. I was more
or less in the centre and twenty yards in front, being the leader.

Then - the machineguns opened up, and we found something like
two or three dozen tanks lined up in front of us, all firing their machine
guns, a line of great grey bulks spitting fire in the darkness. Lines of
golden sparks were crossing and criss-crossing in the air above my
head. I dived for cover, and fell down between the wheatstalks.
German infantry were coming out from behind the tanks into the
wheatfield.

I lay there, frozen with fear in the darkness as a German soldier
approached me and stood, Schmeisser firing over my body at my
friends. He leapt over my body, and others followed. I could do
nothing, only watch, and stay still as a stone. One soldier spotted me,
and called out: "Here is one dead." In the end, the firing died away. I
lay there as they searched, pushing through the wheat all round me,
not daring to move.

Then one of them found me. There was just light enough to see by
now. He was not sure that I was as dead as I looked, and came up and
pointed his Schmeisser right at my head. I stared blankly at the sky, not
daring to even blink my eyelids as he looked at me. While I had been
lying still earlier, I had loaded and cocked my Luger pistol, and taken
off the safety catch. It lay there in my hand as if I had gripped it as I had
fallen, dying. I could see his finger on the trigger of his Schmeisser, and
I made up my mind that if it showed any sign of tightening, I was going
to shoot him and make a run for it.

But I was in luck. His trigger finger stayed relaxed, and someone
called to him: "Leave him there, we'll make the Italians bury him."
The sun was rising. I was lying near a barn full of straw and a field of
wheat. There was still a lot of shooting going on. The shelling stopped

after about twenty minutes, but thousands of bullets and tracer went over my head. I heard orders given to search the area, and someone say: "There is a dead man lying here." I decided not to move, and a German came and shouted: "There is a dead man all right." And he went!

As soon as the sun was high, I decided to look for local farmers who might help me. And there they were, in the bottom of the valley, harvesting the wheat. So I crawled very slowly to the edge of this side of the hill, into the valley, and tucked my sub-machinegun into my trousers, my knees shaking like jelly.

I got up and walked near them, and looked straight ahead, and said: "Don't look at me, just carry on working, and in the meantime, don't say anything." Then I picked up a bunch of straw, put it on my shoulder, and walked normally along the valley and behind the hill, and nobody stopped me. Yet on that hill there were few trees and at least twenty to thirty Germans, who must have seen me.

Behind that hill, there was houses set together, terraced houses. I walked into the first house. The man there was Italian, and I knew him - he had been a partisan. During my early time with the partisans, any person who asked to be relieved from the fighting, and who promised to be loyal to the cause and give no information to the Germans was allowed to go home. This man, who was called Aldo, had been one of these. His father had died, and he had left the mountains to go and support his family. When he saw me, he said: "My God, what are you doing here? They will kill us all."

I said: "I am not staying.... just give me food and something to drink, and I am off." There was a noise just after I finished talking to him. I could hear the engines of armoured cars pulling up in front of the house. They called: "Alles heraus, alles heraus - everyone out, everyone out!"

Aldo asked me what I was going to do, and I told him to carry on, that I was not there and he had not seen me. I was talking to him on the first floor. After that, I quickly climbed out of the window and dropped to the ground at the rear. I knew I would not have a chance if I stayed in there. Behind the house, there was a field of corn on the cob, and I crawled underneath the plants. I could hear everything the Germans said to the Italians. They searched the houses and of course they found nothing. They told them that if they found even a trace of the partisans there, they would kill the lot of them. Looking back on it, I was very lucky. There must have been twenty or thirty Germans up on the hill, and some of them must have seen me go into the man's house. But nobody made the right connections - and it was overlooked. Otherwise, they would have searched till they found me, and that would have been that.

After they had driven away, Aldo came to the window of the house and called: "Giovanni, Giovanni, che va, che va?" I waited, but he kept on, and I called out: "Here." He brought out a big loaf of bread, cheese, some meat, and a bottle of wine, wrapped up in a headscarf. And I went, and I crawled up the hill in an easterly direction, up to the bushes at the top where I could hide.

By now, the sun was setting. I settled down between some of the bushes, very hungry and thirsty. I had a few swallows of the wine and some bread and cheese, and felt better. I went to sleep and woke up, woken by the sound of guns in the mountains. That made me feel better still - up there my friends were continuing the fight. I decided to get moving, and went down the slope of the hill on the other side, going towards a building I could see in the moonlight. A dog barked, and I made a detour and circled the building, and crossed a wood to a ravine, where, between dense bushes, I once again fell asleep.

I was woken by the laughter of women and a man's voice. When I woke up, there was a German officer and four Italian girls, pretty teenagers, having a naked bath in the nearby river. I was at once fit and ready for action. The German had his guns with him, (I could clearly see them, lying on top of his clothes), and we could always use guns. I might as well go back home with something to show for all my trouble.

Well, their clothes were on the other side of the river. So I went a long way round, got on the other side, and crept close, pinched his guns, a Schmeisser and a Luger. I made sure there were no other arms, and then I stood up, and said:

"Are you enjoying yourselves?"

He shouted: "Nicht scheissen, nicht scheissen, don't shoot, don't shoot."

I said: "It depends."

And then one of the girls started screaming, and that was enough for me. I pulled the trigger and emptied the magazine - it was the only way to ensure there were no witnesses to send troops after me. Their bodies settled into the water and all was quiet again.

I went on to the next small hill, and that was on the main road - out of bounds for the German army in the daytime, and I was on the edge of the mountains, my mountains, and I only went a quarter mile up the hill and I was stopped by a partisan guard - a man on sentry duty, but just pretending to be a farmer.

He said: "You've been killed," and I said: "No, I'm still here." And I showed him the German uniform, and the girls' dresses, which I had with me. "Would you like the Iron Cross?" I asked him. He laughed and said he would make do with a wooden one. Then he asked me how I had managed it, and sent a signal to HQ and by the time I managed to get there, I was welcomed by a couple of hundred cheering partisans. They all wanted to look at the German uniform and the decorations, and when Zio came out, he wanted to look at them too.

I asked after my men, and it turned out that they had all got back safely; the fact was that when the tanks had fired on us, we had been breasting a hill. All my men had been hidden safely behind the brow, and only I had been visible. They had retreated before the infantry could catch up with them. But they had seen me falling, and thought me killed. Zio excused me from making an immediate report, as I was so tired, and sent a squad to check on the bodies in the river and dispose of them. One never knew, the local people might suffer if they were found there.

What did I think about killing those Italian girls and an unarmed man? I thought nothing. The Germans killed us whenever they could, and the Italian girls were obviously collaborators. Looking back, I can see that they may have just been young girls, out for a bit of fun with a handsome man - but that is not how one thinks in war - partly because one cannot afford to - it would sent you mad. As it was, I went off and had a very long sleep! I felt I had earned it!

Chapter 12

THE NURSES

Most of the danger I experienced during my time in the partisans
came from German troops on the ground. However, on one occasion I
was in very great danger from the air; and from my own side too!

What happened was this: I was on intelligence duty, working for the
partisan commanders. The Germans were building a bridge in the
vicinity, and I went along to take a look at what they were doing; our
command no doubt was thinking of hindering their progress if
possible. I was pretending to be a farmer, and was strolling along near
Incisa with a scythe over my shoulder, when groups of American
bombers came in from the west, where there were three bridges (which
Zio had shown me on the first day during the journey to the
mountains) and which they intended to bomb. It was a nice sunny day,
between three and four in the afternoon.

The bombers passed over the bridges and went over the mountains
from which I had come, then came round in a big U-turn, going anti-
clockwise, and started to come in for their bombing run with the sun
behind them. I was walking along the main road on top of the hill in
between the bridges, which spanned two parallel valleys. Hearing
engines overhead, I looked up and saw a long black line of bombs
leaving the aircraft and falling towards the bridges.

I jumped into a drainage trench at the side of the road, keeping my
head up and peeking out, watching with great interest to see where the
bombs fell. As the first bomb hit the ground, a huge ball of fire and soil
in the shape of a candle flame erupted and then fell back to the ground.
There were about thirty bombers in all, and their bombs were falling
about a hundred yards from the nearest bridge. As they were crossing
the river (which was the Arno) two of them were hit by German anti-
aircraft fire and one blew up, with only two of the crew parachuting to
safety. The crew of the second aircraft baled out and let their plane,
still burning, to fly on it's own towards the horizon.

The second group of bombers was just approaching the bridge. I
decided to lie down in the bottom of the ditch, in a position which still

allowed me to watch the planes. Seconds after, I could see the bombs leaving the first planes, and as I followed this line with my eyes, I realised that they were falling much closer to me than the previous ones. However, thanks to my good sight (it was very good when I was young) I could calculate that, though close, I need not worry about them yet. I followed the stream of bombs as they fell through the air and hit the ground just in front of the bridge with a series of explosions. A near miss - but still a miss. However, the next lot hit the bridge and did a lot of damage to the lower structure.

The bombers went round and round, each time coming out of the sun as they made their bombing run, so that the eyes of the anti-aircraft crews were dazzled with the light; they went on bombing for about an hour, bombs dropping every two or three minutes. After the first few runs, I noticed that they were beginning to drop bombs very near me. I jumped to my feet and ran - just in time. I had gone about a hundred yards when the first bomb of the next 'drop' exploded a few feet from the position I had just been occupying. I panicked slightly, and tried to run away from the line of bombing.

However, as I was running to my next position, I miscalculated the time of the explosion, and before I came to a stop and dived for cover the blast lifted me into the air, and I landed in a crater from a bomb which had dropped earlier; the soil was still hot from the explosion.

During the gap between one group of bombers finishing their bombing run and the next beginning, I got to my feet and ran as far as possible from the area. At last I considered myself safe, being about five hundred yards away from the line along which the bombs were falling. I sat down beside a big tree, not being aware that about a hundred yards behind me were four 88mm German anti-aircraft guns; in a few minutes these guns came under attack from the air, and once again I had to run for my life. The bombs crashed down behind me and once again, for the second time in just a few minutes, I was lifted through the air by the blast of compressed air released by the explosion.

I actually flew through the air, quite a few feet, and landed in a cornfield, then picked myself up and ran again until I was sure I was at last really safe. Breathlessly, I lay down and peacefully watched the bombs leaving the aircraft and falling towards their targets. After the raid, I walked towards the mountain, and paused when I reached the top of the first hill. From here I had a very good view of the bombing site; both of the bridges and the anti-aircraft batteries. Craters were everywhere, and the guns had been completely destroyed - it was lucky that I had moved so fast. I contentedly made my way back to the partisan HQ in the mountains.

This was a hair-raising experience - but nevertheless, it was straightforward physical danger. Soon I was to have another experience, the horror of which has remained in my mind to this day; an atrocity committed, not by the Germans, but by my own friends and comrades. War is not as black and white as it is pictured, and the fighters of your own side can often commit them as well: that is the terrible truth which I learned that day.

On one occasion, as we mounted what looked like a routine ambush on the East side of the mountain, I found myself leading an attack group of fourteen young men, with six more as a back-up group. We positioned ourself in our ambush - as usual we had chosen a place where there was a sharp bend which slowed down any traffic. For some time we lay there, seeing only an occasional car or light transport. We left these alone, for we knew that these single vehicles were often scouts for a convoy - and even if they were not, they were hardly worth the trouble of a full scale attack.

Towards midnight, an armoured car made it's appearance. It mounted a 40 mm cannon. Far behind it, about a kilometre, we spotted a convoy of light pick-ups and vans. I signalled to the man at the front to leave the armoured car alone, and sent another man to keep a look out down the road where it had disappeared, to give warning if it returned. I was worried lest it should hear the noise of our attack, or even be alerted by radio, and come back to help. With that cannon and it's armour, it could have given us a lot of trouble.

However, we were in luck, and we never saw any more of it. The column of light transports came up to our ambush, and I fired a tracer bullet, our usual signal for attack. There were few soldiers with this column, and the battle was fierce but short. At the end,we found ourselves (unusually) with prisoners on our hands - two high ranking German officers and two women, nurses. We soon found that the men were surgeons and that the convoy was carrying medical supplies, as well as arms and ammunition, to the units in the South. (The invasion of Italy had taken place by this time.)

As we were in desperate need of medical supplies, and had no doctors, I decided that the van which contained medical supplies should not be burnt. I also decided to have the two officers and nurses tied up and blindfolded, and taken to Headquarters in the van. It was

quite a drive. It is actually easier to walk up these mountains than to
drive up them, since there are some many sharp, narrow bends and
near vertical slopes.

As we neared Headquarters, we gave our lookouts a fright.
However, they calmed down when they saw partisans sitting on the
wings, bonnets and roof of the van. On arrival, I told the Commandant
what we had captured. The arms and ammunition alone represented a
very good haul - the largest single consignment that we had captured
for many weeks.

The prisoners had been left sitting on a bench in front of the
building. I had ordered a man to bring them wine, and had ordered
their hands untied after I had personally searched them very
thoroughly for cyanide capsules and arms. I found two tins of cyanide
capsules and tablets, each holding ten. I felt that these might come in
handy, and kept one tin for myself - although this was strictly against
regulations. I just put it in my pocket and did not mention it.

Shortly afterwards, the Commandant came out of the building and
told me to take the prisoners' blindfolds off. They blinked around in
the light, astonished to see so many men carrying German
Schmeissers, grenades and mortars. One of the officers stood up and
saluted the Commandant, and went on to quote his rights under the
Geneva Convention. Our Commandant replied:

"The German Army does not treat our partisans, when captured,
under the Geneva Convention. They shoot or hang anyone who is even
suspected of partisan activity or of any activity which might harm the
Germans. I therefore suggest that you forget all about the Geneva
Convention, and do as you are told." It was decided to put the German
surgeons to work immediately. A clean table was provided as an
operating table, and supplies and equipment were unloaded from the
van. While this was going on, in spite of the Commandant's harsh
words, another table was laid with food and wine, and the Germans
were allowed to refresh themselves.

After everything was ready, and the Germans had finished their
meal, the Commandant ordered some men, chosen for their
intelligence, to stand and watch the Germans at their work, both in
order to keep an eye on them, and also to learn what they could about
their work for the future. The surgeons worked on till nightfall. I went
down to the road that night, and had a successful time, returning with
only two light casualties the following morning. The surgeons were at
work again on the many heavily wounded partisans, amputating limbs

where necessary and patching up as well as they could.

The surgeons stayed with us for ten days, after which their services were requested by some other partisan units, and they were marched off, blindfolded and bound, to work there. I did not see them again. But the two women stayed behind. The Commandant wanted them to go, but the men had their own plans, and refused to let him send the women away.

I knew what was planned and found it sickening. My upbringing was still very strong in me, in spite of the brutalising experiences I had gone through. I hated the Germans, but there were still some things I would not do in any circumstances.

Well, after the departure of the surgeons one morning, it was not long before the younger of the two women found herself stripped and laid on the operating table for another kind of operation. Man after man went up to rape her - in fact, a queue formed. She screamed, cried, and begged to be left in peace, but they took no notice. By late afternoon, she was a terrible sight - black and blue from sadistic beatings during the raping, and blood pouring constantly from her vagina. There was no question of anyone getting sexual pleasure from such a pitiful object - the whole thing was just an exercise in sadism.

As she lay there, one man finished and another ready to take his turn, she called to me, and asked if I spoke German. When I said that I did, she said, "Will you ask them to stop, at least for a while?" I looked at the queue of men and ordered them to stop while I listened to what she had to say. That did not go down well, and one man pulled a gun on me and screamed: "She was given to us - don't dare to stop us!"

I told him: "As long as I am a group leader here, you will obey my orders - put that gun away, or you'll never hold one again." He hesitated, and I stared him right in the eyes - a trick which I had learnt, and which served me well in many tricky situations. It projects your will and determination - and in this situation it helped, of course, that they already knew me as a man who meant what he said.

There were a few tense seconds - then he put his gun away and the queue moved back, leaving me to listen to her. She had little to say, apart from the fact that she had joined the Red Cross a few weeks ago, and had not even been trained as a nurse, but was serving her country as best she could, as we served ours. It was part of her duty to go to the front line, and she had been unlucky, that was all. She asked me to help her in any way I could.

I said: "Would you rather die than let this continue?"

Jan in 1942, eighteen years old, in Podgorodnaja.

Polish group, German labour camp, Podgorodnaja 1942.

Jan, 20 years old, after second mission in Italy, 1944.

Roman Zagurski in German labour camp, Russia 1941.

Jan as a military policeman, Italy 1945.

View from Villa Manichoro, area of Jan's partisan experience.

Jan in the yard of Villa Manichoro (1986).

Omero and his wife, with Jan at Monte Catini (1986).

"Yes," she said, simply.

I said quietly: "I cannot stop the men, but when I come back near you, open your mouth - I will help you." She hesitated, smiled a bitter smile, and whispered her thanks.

I took a few steps away as if I was thinking, and felt in my pocket. I managed to get the tin of cyanide capsules out without anybody seeing them, took one out, and returned to her. I put my hand on her face as if to comfort her. She understood, and opened her mouth, and I pushed the capsule in. A few seconds later, when the first man stepped up to take his turn, she was dead. Nobody realised what had happened. The Commandant presumed that she had died from exhaustion.

The other nurse was kept in the Headquarters building, and I thought that she might be better treated. However, a few days later they threw her out - and she looked forty years older - her eyes demented, shining and wild. As she lay, terrified, on the ground where she had fallen after they had thrown her from the doorway, she saw the men round her coming for her - still hungry for their horrible fun. They shouted abuse and carried her to the table, but she leapt off and ran for the dense bushes and scrub that surrounded the Headquarters building.

I and Zio, who witnessed all this, simultaneously lifted our Schmeissers and fired - intending to send the bullets over her head and frighten her. We were not worried about her escaping. She was in no condition to run far, and we knew the ground very well. However, one of us must have aimed too low, for a bullet carried away a great slab of the front part of her chest, almost disintegrating the whole of her body.

I was terribly upset - these two nurses had been intelligent, well bred women. I tried to console myself by remembering how the Germans had treated Polish women and Russian prisoners of war - the war was a great ocean of suffering, and these two women just drops within it. I felt better - but somewhere inside myself I was not totally convinced.

The cruelties that war gives rise to are almost unimaginable sometimes. On one occasion, I saw a partisan torturing a woman prisoner - just sticking his knife into her breast, her stomach, literally cutting her slowly to pieces. When I asked him why he was behaving like that, he simply said: "She's a Fascist." He was not in my group, and in fact came from another unit on another part of the mountain, so I could do nothing, just turn away.

Some people have asked me how I endured such terrible sights, how I could put up with the horror and still keep functioning. Well, first of all I was really extremely busy - planning ambushes, carrying them out and sleeping often took the whole day and only left me a few hours for sleeping. An exhausted man has little time for emotion - it is a luxury. However, sometimes, when the night's events went smoothly, I had time to myself, and would wander away from the camp, sit down on my own and allow myself to realise what an awful time I was living through.

At such times, as I said above, I comforted myself somewhat by thinking of the way the Germans treated their own prisoners, and of how they, after all, had been the ones to start this terrible war which had brought so much suffering. There I was, still a very young man, stranded far from my family, in constant danger of being killed - and compared to many people, I was lucky. I was not dead, or badly wounded, or in a concentration camp. In the end, I would manage to close my mind to whatever horrors I had witnessed. It was events like this dreadful treatment of the nurses which forced me to be a man of iron, without emotion. If you had felt, you would disintegrate, would begin to make mistakes - and my life and the lives of my men depended on my always being right - this was always my primary concern. After the war I paid very dearly for this suppression of my natural feelings - but that was in the future.

So many terrible things happened - almost daily. On one occasion, not far form Arezzo, we laid our usual ambush. A convoy came along, and we attacked the rear vehicle, a Panzer armoured car, in the usual way. I have said we attacked on bends, since everything had to move slowly there. One man would quietly emerge from the bushes, jump on the back of the moving armoured car, and throw a grenade inside, with another one or two underneath to ignite the tyres.

As the grenades went off, all hell broke loose. Mortars opened up from the other side of the ravine, with 30 mmm machine guns adding to the noise. The Germans had laid an ambush of their own. The position was hopeless. We only had hand grenades, and could not stand up under mortar fire. I ordered a retreat into the mountains parallel to the road to mislead the Germans as to our direction. After the retreat had been completed, I found that my second in command, Giuseppe, was missing.

I went back, keeping out an eye for him. In any case, I wanted to set fire to the convoy - the mortar fire had now ceased, and our fire had killed the crews of all the trucks. When I got back to the road, I found Giuseppe, lying in the road with all his stomach missing. He was in no pain, being still in shock, but I knew, from my experience of such wounds, that he could live no more than two or three hours. He was completely conscious, and he knew, and I knew, that those two or three hours might give the Germans time to break him, and extract a lot of damaging information.

He begged me to take him up the mountain - or, if I could not do that, to kill him. I knew I could not take him with me - moving him with the Germans so near would have been impossible - and in any case, would merely have killed him more quickly. But I could not bring myself to shoot him. However, I remembered my box of cyanide pills. Opening his hand, which was filled with blood, I put a cyanide capsule into it. He did not know what it was, and I told him it would make him sleep.

I think he knew what I really meant. He took my hand and kissed it - which pained me greatly, since I knew that as soon as he took the capsule, he would be gone in a few seconds. I stood by him and he smiled for a few seconds, then put his bloodied hand to his mouth. I walked away, not wishing to see him die - but as I looked back, I could see that he was gone.

Nor was he the only casualty - about a mile and a half from the road, I found another man in such a condition with a leg wound that he could not walk. He was near the outlying houses of a nearby village, but he could not be left there.

I organised things, and sent one of my men to the nearest house to get some strong cognac and what they could find by way of surgical tools; a knife, a saw; for it was obvious that his leg would have to be amputated. My man came back with about five litres of cognac, also a hacksaw, a file, cotton and a needle. We set about getting him drunk straight away - we fairly poured the cognac into him, having laid him out on a flat rock.

Then, as gently and quickly as possible, I cut off his leg at knee level, while he was held still by two others. To this day I do not know how I did it. Actually, he was so drunk that when he woke, he did not even realise, till he looked, that he had lost his leg. Strangely enough, he survived, and I later heard he lived for fifteen years after the war had ended.

Chapter 13

JAN'S GOLD

One night we made an unusual find. The night started in the normal way, an ambush, perfectly successful as most of them were. We ambushed a convoy which was going North, through the passes, towards Germany. After the fighting was over, and the road was littered with bodies, we were looting the convoy as usual, looking for anything we could use. As usual, a few of the Germans were left alive. I and a friend of mine came upon one of them. I suppose he was about my father's age. He knew what was going to happen, and he fell on his knees on the road, begging for mercy, asking for his life.

But the rule was never broken. We both fired at once, and he died, cursing us. I have killed a lot of people, but I shall never forget his eyes, staring at me with hate and fear.

After that, my friend and I carried on looting. Suddenly he called : "How do we open the big steel suitcase?" I went over, and looked at what he had found - a big steel safe on one of the trucks, about four feet wide and four feet deep, and eight long. I said, "Simple, put a few grenades on it and that's it." However, my solution did not work at first. We tried one lot of grenades, and then another. I was a little puzzled. It was a bit too heavy for just an ordinary safe. When they had finished clearing the bodies, I was still working on it, and managed to open it after the fourth lot of grenades, blowing open the hinges.

There were one hundred and fifteen gold bars inside, Italian gold being taken to Germany to help pay for the German war effort. We drove the truck into the mountains, and the Italian colonel took charge of it in the name of the Provisional Government the partisans had declared. Before I left, the Provisional government sent a representative to see me and my colleague, and we got quite a surprise. He gave two bars of the gold to me and my colleague, and four to the local commanders, as a reward for saving the gold for Italy.

Well, of course that was very nice. But it was also an embarrassment. I could hardly carry the stuff around with me. And, as I have said, wealth is dangerous in wartime. In the end, my friend and

I buried it in a deep hollow under a rock on the mountainside, and left it there. Soon after that, he was killed in an ambush, and I was the only one who knew where it was.

However, I was not very much elated by my treasure. The eyes of that man still haunted me, and I had one of my premonitions - they do not come often, are always accurate - that to dig up that gold would mean death - though not necessarily mine.

One of the problems about writing this book has been that I found that I had forgotten many of the things which happened to me; often very remarkable things which at the time I just did not think strange in the bizarre surroundings of wartime. As I wrote, these incidents returned to me. One concerned the ammunition trains.

The partisans constantly received information of one kind and another from the local residents. Among all this were a series of reports from people living in the area of Figline Valdarno that German trains loaded with ammunition were often seen halted between Figline Valdarno and Arrezzo. The railway lines there ran between two high banks and the Germans could hide about four trains at a time there, covered with camouflage nets. I was asked by our commandant to go and investigate the situation and whether the trains could be attacked. This was the kind of job I was generally asked to do, because I spoke fluent German.

In this particular case, I changed into a German uniform and set off on a German motorbike - we had a number of them at partisan headquarters. I also took a forged German pass, and was able to drive straight through German territory. I managed to have a look at the trains without trouble, and went straight back without any incident. It was obvious that the camouflaged trains would have to be destroyed almost immediately, because at night, under cover of darkness, they would be moving south towards the German battle lines.

In the late afternoon, we selected the most reliable and useful men and marched them to the bottom of the mountain, where they boarded civilian trucks for the journey. When we arrived at the railway lines to the south of where the trains were hidden, we mined the lines over a length of two miles (this was on the line which led to Arrezzo), after which we waited for darkness. There was an engine, then a passenger coach for the German officers and soldiers acting as guards; the train was moving very slowly. We waited for the first wagon to pass into the mined area. When the whole train was over the mines, we ignited the explosives under the first wagons by remote control, after which the other mines, which were linked to the first, blew simultaneously, one after another until the whole train was totally destroyed.

That was the first of eight similar operations. We had to be careful not to go too often (even though trains were nearly always waiting in the German hideout under camouflage) because obviously the Germans would be on their guard and would lay in wait for us. However, we always succeeded in the missions we attempted, and each time not only was the ammunition destroyed, but the railway lines were also out of action for several days. This was very inconvenient for the Germans, since this was the only railway connection between Bologna, Florence and Rome.

Chapter 14

JOURNEY TO CAIRO

One day, Headquarters received a message that a number of Allied soldiers escaping from Germany were to be dispatched to another group of partisans in the surrounding mountains of Montecatini - peaks about 4,000 feet high. For the next few days, the Commandant planned routes so that these men could be guided there. From Montecatini the soldiers would have to make their own way with a guide to a fishing village near Porto Ortobello, where arrangements were to be made with the fishermen. The fishermen would then take them along on a fishing trip out on the Tirreno Sea, the stretch of water which lies between Corsica, Sardinia and the Italian mainland.

Once out there, American fighters, which constantly patrolled the area, would spot them and radio to a torpedo boat to come and pick them up. I was involved in the process of helping these escaped prisoners, who were mostly pilots. They were of all nationalities, American, British, Canadian, Australian, French. One day I met one who had a Polish shoulder flash on his uniform. I was very surprised, as I did not know that Poland still had an airforce! In fact, when I asked him if he spoke Polish, I was quite prepared for a negative! However, he was Polish all right, and he told me that he was fighting with the Polish Army in the Middle East.

This surprised me even more - and he told me about the two Polish divisions which had fought for Tobruk and Alexandria together with the British army. Many of the soldiers had come from Russia via Persia, Syria and Palestine - sometimes whole families had come out together. The fact was that Stalin had agreed to release many thousands of men, also women and children, held in Russia after his invasion of Poland. In fact, while I was a Russian prisoner of war, I was, for many months, held contrary to this agreement - for the Russians did not release all the Poles they held.

He asked me to come back with him and fight with my countrymen, and this appealed to me. I had fought hard and well in Italy, but I had seen many things that sickened me, and I could not always approve of the way my comrades had behaved, however well I understood the reasons for it. Also I would naturally prefer to fight with my fellow countrymen. So I went to the Commandant, and asked his permission to leave and go to fight elsewhere. He said that of course I could go, but pleaded with me to explain to the authorities the difficult situation the partisans faced, with a great shortage of ammunition, shortage of medical supplies and clothing, and a great need to be able to communicate readily with Allied planes as they flew overhead, so that messages could be passed to the Allied command.

I was happy to promise to do my best, and memorised the places and times when 'drops' of supplies could be made. A few days later, I said goodbye to my friends among the partisans, and moved down the mountains with the Allied soldiers. As we approached the nearest village we took a careful look around before venturing in to pick up our guide. The guide, who was very experienced in this kind of job, knew the Toscana area very well, and had a truck waiting for us. The truck took us towards Pontasieve and then on to Florence.

Outside Florence, there was a very tense moment. We had to stop at a German patrol point, where all trucks were searched. We were hidden at the front of the truck behind a load of crates containing heavy machinery. However, they were not over-thorough. They opened one crate, and then, finding nothing, waved the driver on. We relaxed - we had been tensed ready for a fight.

We stopped in Florence at a 'safe house' which was the local headquarters of the partisans, situated on the city boundary. Here we were issued with grenades and water proof clothing, and given a substantial meal and a few bottles of wine to keep us warm at night. Late in the afternoon we drove on to Livorno. For several hours there were no incidents, until we were attacked by our own side. British Spitfires came out of the sky and began strafing us with machine guns. The air was filled with the clatter of their fire - we just cursed and lay low. There were a number of trucks travelling together, and though we were not part of the convoy, the Spitfires had no way of knowing that. However, although one truck was hit, ours escaped completely, and at last we reached the village of Ortobello, where we pulled directly onto a quay and into a warehouse. There was a German security guard on the place, but all the staff of the warehouse were Italians, and loyal to the partisans.

At nightfall, the fishing boats which were tied up at the quay prepared for their journey out to sea. As we emerged from our hideout, we were given fishermen's clothing, and one by one we passed the German guards, managed to reach different boats, and pretended to be part of the crew. The boats, with seven pilots and myself, left the port, sailing West towards Corsica. We travelled for several hours, dropping fishing nets on the way. After that, all eight of us were transferred onto the biggest boat, which sailed further south to a rendezvous with Allied planes and torpedo boats.

At daybreak, the other fishing boats were out of sight and there was no sign of land except for some faraway mountains sticking up over the horizon, behind which the sun was rising. It was not long before we heard the noise of aircraft engines coming from the South - it was a plane flying at speed only 50 metres above the sea. We flashed signals to the pilot, and he flew over the boat, slowing down so that he could check us out, and then flew over us a couple of times.

Our captain lit a couple of flares, and the pilot tilted his wings as a signal that he understood and that he had radioed the torpedo boat to come and pick us up. We were nearly safe - the only danger now was a surprise attack from a German submarine or plane, but the fishing captain told us this had only happened once in his experience. However, we were eager to get away, and time passed very slowly. People kept on asking the time. There was nothing to do, nothing at all, and we felt rather frustrated. We were so near to escape to our own people, and it would be heartbreaking if something went wrong at the last moment.

Actually, it was only an hour before we heard the powerful engine of a torpedo boat coming from the Northwest. It approached so fast that we actually thought it was going to pass by without stopping. However, it stopped, and a rope was passed to hold the boats together. We were transferred to the torpedo boat, and our friendly captain got a few presents from the torpedo boat commander. We were told to go below, out of the way, and the Commander of the boat told us that he was only one of nine boats, and that we were to rejoin the others very shortly. Sure enough, as we headed off to the South West, we saw eight dots in the distance, all heading South.

We began to relax and enjoy the food we were served by the crew - when suddenly there was a call "General Quarters" and our hosts had to get ready for action. A submarine had been detected in the area. We still had to stay below, but were told to sit near the exit in case we were shelled. I managed to peep up on deck, and saw all nine boats form a ring. Travelling at high speed, they released depth charges, and one or two torpedoes. They chased each other round and round in a circle continuously as they fired, hoping to elude any torpedoes the submarine might fire in return.

This circling and throwing of depth charges continued for about three quarters of an hour. After this, the submarine surfaced, coming up from underneath the water like a great whale. We thought that it had been hit by a depth charge or a torpedo, and was coming up to surrender. But no such luck. The German captain had obviously become so harassed by the depth charges that he had decided to fight it out on the surface. One against nine sounds long odds, but the fact was that the submarine had a heavy naval gun, much heavier than those carried by the torpedo boats, as well as machine guns.

The torpedo boats opened up with the heavy machine guns which was their only armament apart from their torpedoes. The noise was deafening, and I could see that one of our boats had already been hit on the bow - though not seriously. Then the boat in front of us released two torpedoes simultaneously, and scored a direct hit with one towards the submarine's stern.

Within twenty minutes, the submarine began sinking, it's bow cocking up in the air nearly vertically. A number of German sailors were left in the water - we could not pick them up, as we did not have enough space, but an American destroyer was in the vicinity and would pick them up later. The action was at an end, and the torpedo boats formed themselves in two parallel lines, and made their way off towards the South, and by nightfall we were past Sardinia.

When night fell, all the boats hove to and floated on the surface of the water. One man kept watch, and the rest slept after a substantial dinner. On waking, everyone had a hot drink, and the sailors received their instructions for the day. We were told that a signal had been received the previous night, telling the Commander that there were German transport ships in the area escorted by a cruiser. Apparently, though we did not hear this till later, one of the transports carried a fortune in gold stolen from some of the Middle Eastern countries by the Germans and our torpedo boats were to find the convoy and sink the lot, if possible.

From first light to eleven o'clock, all the torpedo boats spread out in line, several miles apart, to cover as wide an area as possible, looking for the enemy. We had no idea of their course, and so it was a matter of searching blind. The boat just sped along on it's own under an empty sky. At eleven o'clock, however, a signal came in to tell us that the convoy had been spotted by other ships or planes, and telling us where to find them. As we hurried off as ordered, we were not long alone, and were soon in company with two of our comrades. And soon after that, we rejoined the rest of the flotilla, all heading in one direction - West. Very soon, we could see the masts of four ships heading North West. Action was imminent.

The torpedo boats, which were travelling in two parallel lines, spread out to form one long line, side by side, about a mile between each boat. They were lined up on the East side of the convoy at a distance of about 15 kilometres. The sailors on our boat made sure that the tubes were loaded and that everything was ready, then, after an exchange of flashed signals between the boats, their engines revved to maximum power. The noses of all the boats lifted into the air, and we charged down on the German ships.

We moved so fast on the calm sea that they seemed to grow larger by the second. Hardly quickly than it takes to talk of it, we were in torpedo range, and also within range of their armament. All the guns they had opened up on us, and shells were exploding all round our boat. It was probably worse for us than the sailors, for they had work to do while we could only sit tight - but very thrilling at the same time.

Machine gun bullets stitched the water in front of us - but none of the boat Commanders took any notice, or looked to see if any of their friends had suffered - the only thing in their minds was the damage they could inflict on the enemy.

As soon as we were close enough to have a really reasonable chance of a direct hit, two torpedoes leapt from the tubes on each boat, and then the whole flotilla, boat by boat, swerved and drove towards the other side of the convoy at varying distances, so that the gunners on the German ships could not get the range. Then they began to circle the German ships like Indians round a wagon train, waiting for another opportunity to strike.

The sailors worked like maniacs to reload the tubes - we passengers were able to help in this, and ease the crew's work. They were glad they had us on board, for the torpedoes were very heavy, and had to be manoeuvred by hand and winch.

By the time the boats turned again towards the convoy, we heard the explosions coming from a number of direct hits. Every ship in the convoy had been hit, in fact, and they were slowly going down. However, the German cruiser, though ablaze, was still floating, and so two more torpedoes were fired into her to make sure of her destruction.

While the ships slowly sank, the torpedo boats raced round and round them in a large circle out of reach of their armament. As the last one went down, a cheer arose from each boat in the flotilla, and they formed two lines, as previously, and headed South East. Towards the end of the afternoon, we were told that the torpedo boats' mother ship was in to the neigbourhood and we were to receive torpedoes, ammunition and fuel for a further journey. We were eager to get to Egypt, but the Commander of our boat said: "Oh, we'll get there, but first of all we have to carry out our immediate job." The mother ship was a Victory class type of transport ship, and all the torpedo boats came alongside her and received more torpedoes. Four of the passengers on our boat were transferred to another, to leave more room for the crew on ours.

We had just completed refuelling and stacking the torpedoes when two German fighters, high on the horizon, started to line up for an attack. The torpedo boats spread out rapidly to circle the mother ship. The German fighters made one low level run, and then machine-gunned the mother ship. However, our torpedo boats filled the sky with their own machine gun bullets, and shot down one of the German fighters.

The second fighter came in to attack the mother ship again, but was received with heavy fire and dived into the sea. The pilot parachuted to safety, and was made prisoner on the mother ship. The incident was over, and we formed into line ahead and moved off Eastwards. Once again, during the night, the men went to sleep and the boat just floated quietly on the calm sea. The next day we went on heading East, and the pilot told me, although he had not been told so, that we must be heading for Egypt.

However, my sea adventures were not completely over. About lunch time, a squadron of Spitfires came over, high above us, and circled several times - and one fighter detached itself, came down low and dropped a floating canister with an orange marker. We picked it up, and the message informed the Commander of our flotilla that there was a German submarine on the surface near us. If we made off at top speed we could be there in twenty minutes. At once, we formed up in a single line and went directly into the attack. The submarine was still on the surface when we arrived - but swiftly dived when it spotted us. The torpedo boats began to go round in tighter and tighter circles until they were only a few hundred metres apart, and then started to drop depth charges.

Soon after, debris began to appear from under the sea, followed by a tremendous explosion which lifted thousands of tons of water from the centre of our circle of boats. After that, bodies began to float to the surface, first a few, and then many, most of them alive - no doubt they had managed to get out via the escape hatch. We left them to be picked up by larger craft - they would be none the worse for a little salt water. One of our boats had engine trouble, and had to be towed, and we had to make for the nearest port, steering South East.

The next two days and nights passed very quietly - the only diversion being the passing of several British and American convoys, each one of which greeted us with cheers. And so, nine days after we had been handed over to the navy by the fishing boats, we headed in to a smudge of land on the horizon - Port Said.

Everyone was happy - the whole atmosphere was very pleasant and relaxed. But in my own mind, I was full of mixed feelings. I could not quite believe that after all these years, I would be finally free and back in a civilised world surrounded by Allies - and perhaps even be once more in the Polish Army. But it was true - and I shall never forget seeing Polish uniforms and Polish shoulder flashes and markings on the quay when we pulled into Port Said. For the first time since 6th September, 1939, I was truly a free man.

Chapter 15

KILLER TRAINING

As we disembarked at Port Said, we were met with welcoming parties - each to meet their own nationals. The Polish pilot who had told me of the existence of the free Polish forces, and thus decided me in favour of escaping from Italy, was met by a Polish captain. After giving him his rank, squadron and number, he introduced me:

"This is Mr. Maslany, an ex-prisoner of war among the Russians, who was also captured by the Germans in the Ukraine. He escaped from Bavaria to Italy, where he has been serving for several months with the Italian partisans." He then went on to add: "He also helped numerous Allied soldiers, who were escaping from Germany via the Italian mountains, to reach Egypt, by which means many were able to rejoin their units to continue their fight for the cause." The Captain shook my hand and told me that there would be plenty of opportunities for me, and invited me to join the Polish Forces. However, first of all, he told me that I would have to attend Polish Headquarters for a simple interrogation as to the most suitable duty for me.

I asked him what the chances were of my joining a Polish fighter squadron, to which he replied that that was not his decision, so he could make no comment. We drove off in the inevitable jeep for Cairo. The conversation continued, and I was so excited with the prospect of the chances before me, and my new status, that I hardly noticed the journey, which ended at the Royal Hotel. Things had been well organised, and when I went to my room I found a complete set of new clothes, plus three pairs of shoes of varying sizes - I just had to select the ones that fitted me. New clothes, new shoes - what a wonderful feeling.

Moments later, the bedside phone rang, and I was asked to come down to the American Bar, which I found in the basement. There I found a Captain and two Lieutenants of the Polish forces, and seconds later my friend the Polish pilot and his squadron leader appeared. After a couple of drinks, we went in to dine - the service was terrific, and the food top class. A good meal - such an ordinary thing, but something which I had gone without for so long. I wanted to order everything on the menu, but realised that I would be very sick if I ate too much, for my stomach, half-fed for so long, just was not up to it. Instead, I settled for a simple meal. After that, the pilot and myself got to bed for a good rest, since we were to move on the next day.

Next day, breakfast was substantial. (Once again, I realise that I always emphasise food throughout this book - but only because it assumes such importance when you do not always have it!) Afterwards, I said goodbye to my friend the pilot, who wished me luck and hoped that we would meet again. I thanked him for his advice and help, and saw him off in an R.A.F. jeep.

As for me, I had to wait a further hour before I was collected by a Lieutenant, who explained the complicated procedure of interrogation and 'de-briefing' that awaited me. The main object was to be sure of my identity. He told me I was not to be afraid to tell the truth, whatever I had had to do to escape; the truth would never be held against me. I suppose this was standard advice, since many people had committed crimes in the heat of war which they later feared to reveal. The journey took several hours; we went to a camp outside Cairo, a transit camp surrounded with a barbed wire fence and guarded at the entrance, although the gates were wide open. For a split second it reminded me of a Labour Camp such as I had been confined in in Russia.

Either the Lieutenant was unusually sensitive, or my dismay registered very plainly on my face, for he assured me that the fence was not to keep those inside in, but those outside out. The local Arabs would have been all over the camp, trading with the Polish soldiers and either cheating or robbing them, if precautions had not been taken. When we drew to a halt, the Commanding Officer, a Major Shyska, approached us.

"We have a new arrival, is that correct?"

"Yes, sir." I replied, and he gently asked me to follow him to his office. They were all obviously accustomed to receiving badly shocked and upset people whose whole lives had been shattered, for they were all very tactful. He then started to question me, and the usual official rigmarole of dates, places, relations' names, dwelling places, etc., was all put down on paper. I was then advised to change my name, since, it was pointed out, if I fell into German hands my family might be punished for my fighting against them. I decided I would adopt the name of Jan Sokolowski - this name had belonged to a schoolfriend of mine.

I told him about my educational qualifications, and emphasised my three years' training in the Central Technical College at Lwow, and my possession of an Ordinary National Certificate in Aero Dynamics. The Major was quite impressed, and told me that, if I wanted to advance my education further, the Army provided crash courses. The Major's attendent sergeant, who had been taking notes of the interview, then handed me over to a corporal, who took me to a tent, and told me to collect my army clothing in one hour. There were six other men there in the tent, some of whom had been there for several days, and others only for a day or so. In due course we collected identity cards, were assigned numbers, and were issued with British Army uniforms with Polish insignia. After there was lunch - both substantial and tasty.

For the next six days we marked time, amusing ourselves during the day with football or other exercise, while in the evening there were daily films on a large field screen; which I enjoyed very much. At the end of the six days, we were lined up on parade, and the Sergeant-Major in charge told us that the transit camp now held six hundred men, and it was time for various high ranking officers to come and pick out individuals for various units. However, specific requests for transfers would be considered, subject to the needs of the army and our abilities and health.

The officers arrived shortly after in a convoy of five or six jeeps, which pulled up in the centre of our square. The first one to make the rounds was a tall, well built man, a Colonel, who simply stared. It was rather disconcerting - he just looked into the eyes of selected individuals, sometimes only for a few seconds, and sometimes longer and more deeply. Most often, he made no comment, but just moved on. But every now and then, without a word, he would point to a man he had just looked over, and the Sergeant-Major would tell that man to step out as the Colonel moved on. Sixty six men were picked out in this way out of the six hundred present, and when Colonel Starski (for that was his name) finished he ordered the selected men to form three lines and follow the Sergeant-Major. I was among them.

We were sent in a truck to another camp, a few miles away, virtually empty apart from kitchen and training staff. We were given sleeping quarters, four men to a tent, bedding, and mosquito nets. After dinner, there were films on another field cinema. Nobody said anything of why we were here, but we were told that general instructions would be issued the next day. However, as we were being told this (during our reception briefing) I asked permission to speak to the Staff Sergeant, and said I would like to join an R.A.F. fighter squadron. He said he would see what could be done.

We had been issued with rifles and ammunition, which we kept to hand. However, the Germans had by then been driven out of North Africa, and we did not seriously expect trouble. However, at 4.3O a.m., the alarm rang! We jumped out of bed, totally unprepared, frantically disorganised, and tried to get dressed while grabbing our arms. The Sergeant-Major was calling from outside, telling us to get outside, never mind about our dress, just line up as quickly as possible.

When we got outside, we found the Sergeant-Major and the Lieutenant in charge standing there with stop watches. They began to abuse us, very loudly, for our complete lack of preparedness, and told that we were lucky it had only been a training alarm. Our training had already begun - we were sent back to our tents, and told that we were to be on parade in half an hour - we had some running to do. With that, the Lieutenant dismissed us with a "Good morning," and vanished to his quarters. Perhaps I ought to have taken a hint from the way the camp was arranged, with the tents pitched behind banks of evacuated soil so as to be unseen, while on the North side, the camp was concealed behind trees and waterlogged ditches.

Everyone was on parade half-an-hour later, and we began running. The bugle sounded, and formed up in gym gear, under the instructions of a Sergeant Major PT instructor, who led us off on a gruelling run of about a mile. On return, some men were completely exhausted, and slumped on their beds, unable to move. I was not among them; I had become accustomed to long marches and strenuous exertion and I still felt quite well, and made off to the field showers for a refreshing clean-up, after which I made my way to the field kitchen for the next thing on the menu - food! I was the first there, but was soon joined by others, especially the other men who, like myself, had become toughened by their experiences.

The morning was taken up with an intelligence test, and after lunch we were given arms instruction, and issued with new automatic rifles, straight from the warehouse and covered with grease and greaseproof paper. These, of course, had to be cleaned, and the Sergeant said: "This job is to be done tonight to make you relax, and tomorrow morning, when I inspect your weapons, God help anyone who fails to show me a perfect job." This man used to have a saying which he often trotted out: "As long as the job is done perfectly it is good enough."

A hard evening's work followed - and by the time the rifles were totally clean and in good order we were indeed tired. Hardly had our heads touched the pillow when the bugle was sounding again, it was 5 a.m., and we were turned out for another mile run - and we were told we had to cut two minutes off yesterday's time. This daily run was a routine for the next six days.

Nor did the training let up - mostly field combat training, during which live ammmunition was fired over our heads. They really put us through it, and very often we hardly had the energy to collect our lunch. Several men dropped out through lack of stamina. During the third week, we learned judo and jujitsu, also details of the human nervous system, and various methods of murdering a man with your bare hands. During these practice combats - which were carried out with our friends - we were only allowed to surrender when, if the fight had continued, death would have resulted. This week weeded out another twelve men.

The fourth week brought more combat training, in the mornings, while the afternoons were given over to intellectual training - this time in Polish law and justice. Through all this time, we were not allowed out of the camp, indeed we were not even allowed to circulate freely within the camp itself, but had to keep to our own part of it. It was emphasised that our training was strictly private. At this time I asked the Staff Sergeant, casually, about my request for transfer to an R.A.F. fighter squadron, but he made no comment, just told me to do my best at what I was doing, as one day my life might depend on it.

I replied that I already knew on what my life depended from my experiences in the partisans' camp. He stopped speaking for a few seconds, and then said: "You are a lucky man, as you must realise..... to have learnt these things," and then walked away.

After two weeks, we were told that we would be going to a refresher course in foreign languages. However, not all of us were to go. Twenty-seven men had not passed the course, and were discharged. I was amongst those retained. Our future duties were still a mystery - nobody ever mentioned what they might be, though occasionally mysterious remarks were made, giving vague hints. Before the new course began we had a free weekend - and were warned once more to discuss our training with nobody.

The following Monday, two lorries carted us off to a town on the outskirts of Cairo, where we were set to study Russian, German, and Italian. Of course, this was fairly easy for me, since I already spoke fluent Russian and German, and knew quite a bit of Italian from my experience in the mountains. However, there was still room for improvement in my German and Italian grammar, and I studied hard. At the end of the course, nine more of us were failed, and we were now only eighteen in number. The course ended on a Friday, and in the late afternoon, we were called in to face the Polish Provost Marshall, who said:

"Gentlemen, please be seated. I would like to introduce you to a British Officer from British Headquarters; because for the next two weeks or thereabouts, you will be directly under his command, to help him with his duty."

His first command was to take our equipment, except for our rifles, and follow him to waiting trucks. We drove into the desert to his Headquarters, a badly bombed building, which, however, he had managed to make comfortable and pleasant. We were then joined by two British lieutenants, who instructed us in German:

"Near here, within a radius of thirty kilometres, there are still German deserters and remaining units who have not surrendered. Our duty is to capture them and take them to a prison camp. It is also more than likely that you will find some Italian soldiers. However, unless they are Fascists, they will not cause you any trouble. Be prepared to leave at 1800 hours with a platoon of British and Polish soldiers, and a British officer to guide you in the desert; as you are newcomers you will find the desert unfamiliar and difficult." And that was it. We were reminded once again to be ready at 1800 hours, and also that iron rations and special desert clothing would be issued before departure, and we were all responsible for making sure everyone had everything.

At nightfall, we set off in several jeeps fitted with silencers and mounting heavy machine guns. Darkness came very quickly, but there was a bright half moon. We headed south west, showing no lights, and without any noise except for the exhaust pipes, which emitted a faint whisper which was inaudible only a few yards away.

We travelled slowly, at about 15 or 20 kilometres an hour, moving like ghosts through a moonlit desert landscape. However, this clear visibility was deceptive. The desert was not flat, but lay in an endless series of swelling mounds, and in between these mounds lay areas of shadow which could conceal anything.

At one point, the British officer who was our guide stopped the column and called the leaders of the jeeps, of whom I was one, together. We were given maps with directions and instructions to help us avoid danger, for we were about to separate. We were to sweep out across the desert and look for the enemy, reassembling at 0600 hours at the point from which we had started. Radio silence was to be maintained except in emergency, since some of the German units for which we were looking were supposed to have radio equipment which they might use to intercept our broadcasts.

I set off, travelling directly south, very slowly, in order to run the engine as quietly as possible. We had travelled for about two kilometres when we spotted the shadows of four men outlined against the sand in the moonlight. My men left the jeep and quietly surrounded the area; soon one of them returned to tell me that the four men we had seen were all that there were, and that they were Italians.

I told my men to capture them as quietly as possible. The four men were now strolling towards our stationary jeep, but in a few minutes they were surrounded by the shadowy forms of my men. For a few moments there was confusion, but no shooting, and the four Italians surrendered. There was a lieutenant, two sergeants and a private. The only one who was armed was the lieutenant, who handed over his gun.

We took them with us, which made the jeep very crowded, and continued to comb the area. After two hours, we sighted a small fire, giving out little or no smoke, just a spark on the desert floor, with several people huddled round it. We had to tie the Italians up and leave them there on the sand while we investigated.

We crawled near the fire, and listened to the conversation. There were several men lying there asleep, as well as two or three awake and on guard. From the talk, they seemed to be a mixture of Germans and Italians. I spread out my men round the camp, and told them to attack when the headlights of the jeep were turned on.

When they were all in position, I turned on the headlights of the jeep, so that they shone directly onto the group round the fire. This dazzled them, and their surprise was so great that they surrendered without any resistance.

This meant that there were too many men to ride in the jeep, and therefore I ordered them to march in a column behind it, about thirty of them, with a couple of my men acting as guards. At about 4 a.m. we reached the place where we had left the four Italians, and ordered them to join the column after we had untied them. After that we went back to the rendezvous point, to find that almost every group had made some captures, and there were about two hundred German and Italian prisoners in the bag. Radio silence was broken to request transport for them, and it arrived about half-an-hour later. Soon the prisoners were on their way, having been thoroughly searched, with us following in convoy.

On arrival back at the camp the Commanding Officer congratulated us on a very successful night's work; we were told that the number of prisoners taken in this way each night was constantly dwindling as the last remnants of Rommel's army and the Italian forces were rounded up.

The next day, we learned that eight further men had been failed and sent off the course, leaving only ten of us. We were also told that the next phase of the training would be the most severe, and would start at 0600 hours the following day, but not in the camp. In the event, we were taken by jeep to an airfield south west of Cairo, and were introduced to Wing Commander Ted Gibson, the Commanding Officer. He explained to us: "You are going to learn to fly and eventually you will learn to fly every type of aircraft here. However, your first training will be on the Tiger Moth. Everyone must pass solo on this aircraft, and only those who manage to do that in less than six hours will pass the test."

We were given some preliminary instruction on the take-off procedure on all the types of aircraft on the airfield, and were then issued with take-off kit and each sent up in a Tiger Moth with an instructor in each plane. After I had flown four hours with the instructor, I was told that I was ready to fly solo. That was really a thrilling moment; the aircraft, being loaded with only one person's weight, took off in half the distance it had before, and climbed very rapidly to 1,000 feet. Rather to my surprise, I had an excellent flight and managed a perfect landing. I had an hour's rest after that, and then we continued.

After this my flying progressed very fast, and before the day had ended I had flown solo on four different types of aircraft - a crash course indeed, but that was how things worked in wartime; courses that would normally have taken weeks or months were crammed into much less time. It was very hard work, and we all had to concentrate fiendishly on getting everything right first time. That evening it was no surprise to learn that four more men had failed and left the course. The six who remained, including me, were told that we were to stay on for two more days, and learn to fly different types of aircraft. Of course they said that the standard we would reach would not entitle us to a pilot's licence, but it would enable us to fly all kinds of aircraft in emergency, for example if we were in enemy territory and got a chance to steal a plane, so as to escape in an emergency.

The following Friday, each of the six class survivors were given flying certificates to testify to our abilities, and the Wing Commander said goodbye to us. On return to Cairo, we found more work waiting for us - books in German and Italian to read - out loud, over and over again, out loud, so that our pronunciation improved. This monotonous work continued for two days, after which we were sent to another airfield; this time, to learn parachuting.

The first step was jumping inside the hanger, on ropes, before we graduated to the real thing. The instructor helped us put on our parachutes and check them for safety. He then put on one himself and we went out to a DC3, parked with it's engine running. Once on board, we strapped ourselves to the benches which were specially fitted for paratrooper use, and waited for the order to latch up our jumping lines. We had to watch a light fitted inside the fuselage - the jumping light. When it glowed red, we were to standby, and be ready, and when it was green, we were to jump. Soon after, we were at 8,000 feet, and told we were to jump on safety lines with a breaking strain of 25 kilograms. (It is far from easy to pull open your own parachute in mid air, and this is normally only done when absolutely necessary, or when the first chute fails. A safety line, which does the whole thing automatically, pulling out the parachute before breaking, is the usual procedure.)

The really terrifying part of parachuting is actually leaving the plane. A baby comes into the world, they say, with only two pieces of inbuilt 'programming' - fear of bright lights and fear of falling. To jump into mid-air is a totally unnatural thing to do. Most people have to be pushed, and I was no exception. I hesitated for a moment, but then there was a hand on my shoulder, and I was floating over the desert.

The strange thing is that once you leave the plane, the fear ceases. The parachute opens, you float down. As I hit the soft sand that first time, it seemed like a joy ride. We did five more jumps, and I no longer had to be pushed out.

After which, it was back to headquarters once again. Our training was over, and the future was uncertain. How were we to be used? Actually, I was not worried about that at the time. I just wanted some rest - parachuting is a very emotionally exhausting business - especially the first time!

Chapter 16

THE FIRST MISSION

However, I did not get my sleep. When I arrived back at headquarters, I had only got to my tent and just managed to undress, when the Sergeant Major came in with a very serious expression on his face. He handed me a map, and told me that I had to stay in my tent and study it. Nobody else must see it or be told of it's existence, and at 0600 hours the following morning I was to report to Polish Headquarters. All my belongings were to be bundled up and left in the stores for safekeeping.

He finished up by smiling broadly, and saying I must be going on holiday - but I knew better. My training had fitted me for special duties, and one had come up sooner than I had expected. Instead of going to sleep, I studied the map until a jeep arrived to take me to Headquarters. There I was taken directly to the Chief Intelligence Officer.

As I waited in his outer office, I began to wonder whether there was something wrong. Perhaps they had made some mistake when checking up my past, and I was under suspicion. Or had I done something wrong, opened my mouth too much or broken some regulation? My guilty conscience worked overtime. However, before I could torture myself too much, a lieutenant came out and told me that the Chief Intelligence Officer would see me right away. He greeted me very pleasantly, shook my hand, invited me to sit down, and offered me a drink. Then he said:

"We are now one Army; we have one common enemy, and whether the British, Americans, Australians, Canadians or any other of the allies require our services, we will always oblige them. When you leave this office, you will be driven to meet another officer under whose command you will serve."

He went on to speak at great length; he went over my past experiences with the Russians, the Germans and then with the partisans, refreshing my memory and reminding me what kind of enemy I was fighting. He concluded by pouring two glasses of vodka, and made a toast: "To the complete success of the mission you are undertaking, and to seeing you back here again very soon." He drank and then we had another glass - "This is to you and I and to good luck." We shook hands and I left, to find my driver waiting for me.

I was off to war again - but this time as Jan Sokolowski. I had a different service number and a completely new identity, with a different age and place of birth. On the journey, I was rather disconcerted when the corporal addressed me as 'Sir', since I had no rank - and my shoulder flashes were rather anonymous, bearing on the words: HQ STAFF on a green background. My mysterious mission seemed to be already making me into an important person.

After a journey of several miles into the desert, we came to the edge of a hill. Below, we could see tents and barrel-shaped barracks camouflaged to hide them from the air. When we stopped, the driver asked me to go into the barracks nearby, and take the second door on the right. This I did - quite unprepared for what happened. Everything seemed very normal, and I was quite off my guard.

When I knocked on the door, I heard the word "Enter". This was slightly odd, since I was expecting a command in Polish. However, I went straight in; if I was to meet an officer from another army, there was all the more need to show myself as a Polish soldier trained to obey orders with the highest discipline. But when I went in I found myself face to face with:

A German officer! He wore a major's uniform, and had his back turned, looking through the window. My first thought was that I had somehow been tricked into a secret German camp. And I had no arms except for a personal combat knife! I stood there, unable to move, for quite a few seconds, until the German Major turned round and said loudly in German: "Are you going to stand there all night saying no word as to who you are, what you are and why you are here?"

I was terribly tense, and managed to stammer in German that I had made a mistake and had got lost. I babbled on and on for nearly five minutes before he laughed and said, in Polish, "You'll do just fine."

"Are you Polish?" I gaped at him.

"Of course, we are in the Polish army, I am Johann Kruger." He then ordered me to go across the hall to the next room and dress myself in my new uniform; I still did not know what was going on, since I was wearing a new uniform anyway - crisp and just issued. However, when I got across the hall, there was a German uniform waiting for me - a Major's uniform with the insignia of an Eastern front Panzer division, above which hung an Iron Cross. Beside the table on which it lay was a batman, standing to attention. He spoke in Polish:

"I am here to help you, sir, and advise you about the instructions written on this piece of paper. From now on you are Major Hoffman, who was badly injured at the Russian front and is just about to begin a spell of convalescence in Germany. The rest of your instructions will be given you on the flight by Major Kruger, whom you have already met." He handed me the paper and I began putting on the uniform. My mind was in a whirl at the turn of events. When I had escaped from Bavaria, about a year before, I had sworn that I would never, under any circumstances, be back. Yet now, on my first mission for the Allies, I was going back to Germany. I could not suppress nervous twitches and tremors running through my body. It took all my past experience to remain calm. Now I understood why the Chief Intelligence Officer had insisted on giving me a drink.

The batman checked out my uniform, and issued me with a German Luger pistol and fifty rounds of ammunition together with all the papers and documents to authenticate my identity and rank. They were all genuine - no doubt they had been taken from some Major captured or killed in Russia. The batman said: "Herr Major, you are now ready to see your colleague across the hall."

I could hardly take in what was happening to me. I entered the room I had walked into only a few minutes before in British uniform - but now I was a German officer, complete in every detail. Major Kruger rose, stretched out his right arm and said: "Heil Hitler." I hesitated only for a split second, then stood to attention, snapped out my right arm, and gave him "Heil Hitler." straight back.

"Zer goud," laughed Major Kruger, "Very good. From this moment, we speak only in German - no mistakes. If there is any Polish or any other language to be used, leave it to me - no-one is to know that you are anything other than German."

After a final check, we marched out to a waiting jeep, and drove off west to where a Dakota DC3 was waiting for us. It had American markings. We were the last people on board, and the fuselage was partitioned off so that the people in front could not see us. Minutes later we were airborne, and Major Kruger opened his map and told me what I was to do.

The mission he described was simple and brutal. A man had to be killed; a man who was a double agent, and working more for the Germans than for us. The local people were not trusted to do this job, and also I was to bring back some papers with me that this man would have in his possession.

Well, I had killed quite a lot of times before, but never like this. My stomach was full of butterflies, and I could not calm my nerves. What made things a lot worse was the fact that I could do nothing but just sit and wait while the plane droned on. It was several hours before the pilot told us that we would be over our 'jumping ground' in fifteen minutes. Major Kruger and I put on our parachutes, and the doors were opened. A last check - thirty seconds to go. On came the green light, and Major Kruger pushed me out of the door - he did not wait for me to jump. Maybe he had had experience of last minute nerves before.

We floated down to the earth together, to make an uneventful landing in a field. We had hit our target exactly - and there was a German car with a German sergeant waiting for us. Our Intelligence people must have alerted them by radio to expect us. Major Kruger told me that we were to part company. He was going on a different mission of his own. However, he still regarded me as his protegé and when the driver dropped me off at my destination, he shook hands and gave me a last bit of reassurance and advice: "See you in Cairo - you will be contacted. Don't look for anything here, remember you are convalescing."

The car drove away - I was left in front of a huge mansion which had been converted into a hotel and requisitioned as an officers' convalescent home. I was in Southern Germany. I walked up the steps and went in. A room had already been booked for me, and my whole path smoothed and made plain. Everything was going exactly according to plan, but I was still terribly nervous. I was sitting in a hotel in the middle of enemy country; I was alone, and completely dependent on myself. I could not stay in my room all the time, and had to be careful to always walk about like a cripple. There were plenty of other officers, many of high rank, staying at the hotel, and they continually pestered me with questions about the Russian front. My instructions had foreseen this, however, and I had to maintain the pretence that I was a very rude, temperamental person. To all their questions I made the same reply: "If you want to know about the Russian front, I would suggest you go there yourself and find out." Then I would just walk away, leaving them very unhappy with my rude behaviour.

This went on for two days. Then, on the second day, a Mercedes, driven by the same man who had dropped me there earlier, pulled up at the hotel. He still wore his sergeant's uniform. He sought out the officer in charge and asked permission to speak to me. In front of everyone, he saluted and politely informed me that Headquarters required my presence. I was very thankful to leave the hotel and those constant questions. We drove to a house outside town where I was to meet the double agent I was to kill. He was called Hanz Schwaizer, and was expecting my call, and thought it was just a routine visit by an Intelligence contact.

When we got there, he invited me in, but I said: "We have much more important things to do than make conversation - just follow me, please." We drove away, and he seemed to suspect nothing. I was sitting in the back with him, but I kept my eye on the driving mirror. When I saw the sergeant nod his head, I knew that he was going to take me to the place where the killing was to take place, remote enough for no-one to hear shots. He drove deep down a quiet side road. Schwaizer (who had behaved quite normally up to then) became very nervous. I asked him what the matter was, and he asked where we were going.

I said that we needed to have a very confidential conversation, with no fear of being overheard. This seemed to satisfy him, and soon after that, I asked the sergeant to stop the car, as we wished to go for a walk. As we moved away, I managed to fall a few steps behind him, and at once reached to pull my Luger from the holster.

But Schwaizer had not been completely deceived. No doubt he had a bad conscience, and realised that the elaborate precautions we had taken to avoid company and witnesses meant only one thing. Even as I reached for my gun, he must have realised that he was in danger. He began to turn, pulling his gun out as he turned. But he was not quite quick enough. I fired three shots into his head to make sure of him. He slumped down by the side of the road, and I quickly went through his clothes, taking all his papers and some cyanide capsules he had hidden away in special hidden pockets.

My mission was accomplished, and the sooner I was away the better. We drove back to the main road and off - straight for Switzerland. We reached the border in about four hours driving. I had to pass the frontier, and went past the German guards without difficulty. I then showed my German military identification papers at the Swiss border post.. Everything was in order, but the Swiss border guard told me that I was not allowed to wear German uniform in Switzerland. Fortunately, my driver was prepared, and had a suitcase with him with a change of civilian clothes for me. I changed in the car, (we were still on the stretch of road between the two border posts) and passed over into Switzerland, saying goodbye to my driver, who had to go back to Germany with the car.

There were several thousand francs of Swiss money in my suit pocket (the driver had thought of everything) and I took a taxi to St. Moritz. I spent the night there, and then, the next day, took another taxi to the Italian border. I crossed the frontier without difficulty and walked to the nearest village, from which it was a short walk into the mountains.

I slept in the open that night, and studied the instructions given to me before I left Cairo. I now had to make contact with the partisans again. It was cold that night, and when day came I tried to warm myself by walking up and down. I could see the mountain peak towards which I had to travel, and all that day I made my way cautiously across country. Actually, I felt a lot better - coming to Italy was like coming home, and the deeper I got into Italian territory, the easier I felt.

Finally, I heard a noise up ahead in the woods. I hid in the bushes and saw four partisans walking towards me. I waved a white handcherchief over my head and called out in Italian. Four guns were soon pointing at my head, but the men allowed me to approach, hands held high. I showed that I knew my way around by describing and naming the Commandant of the partisans of Monte Giove and the Commandant of the mountains round Figline Valdarno, and they decided to take me to their own Commanding Officer.

My identity was quickly confirmed, and I had no further trouble, and was passed from one group to another till I reached my old command, and met my old Commanding Officer. After a lot of talk, I was given an Italian uniform and was taken by road to Ortobello. Once again, I boarded a fishing boat and was taken out to sea for another journey by motor torpedo boat - an American one this time.

Three days later, I was back, facing the Chief Intelligence Officer in his office! All had gone well - that is, if successfully shooting a man in the back of the neck while pretending to be his friend was success. And my reputation as a cool killer was made. My superiors thought that I was a natural killer, a man who could eliminate people in cold blood without any worry or remorse, a man of steel nerves. How wrong this was! On each of my missions I was in a continuous state of nerves and tension, though I did not show it - how could I, when my very life depended on my appearing normal at all times. I have always been a self-disciplined man - my early family life and devotion to study saw to that. But truly, looking back at it, it might have been very much to my advantage if I had been a man who showed his fear and unhappiness more openly. If I had been, I would not have been selected for these jobs at all. My outward composure and calm thus led to some truly horrendous experiences later on. I did not think of all this at the time, however. I was just glad to be safely back!

Chapter 17

POLICE WORK

After I had come back from the first mission, I was sent back to ordinary duties, and this involved my going to Africa, a journey which I made several times.

Stalin agreed, after he allied himself with the British and Americans, that he would let go all the Polish prisoners he had held. In fact, he should have let me go - the agreement took place while I was still a prisoner. But he did not. However, he did release many Poles from Southern Russia, who were released via Persia (Iran as it is now) and moved via Syria and Palestine down to Cairo. From there they were sent down to Salisbury, in Rhodesia, were settled into camps, and assessed. The old people and children were generally left there. But the young adults were re-trained and drafted into the Free Polish Army which was forming and expanding.

I went along with the convoys as a security man. Many of the released Poles were bad lots, I am afraid to say, either criminals whom the Russians did not want, or people who had become dangerous and depraved because of the war and what they had suffered.

I had been assigned to work with another two military policemen, Henryk Krulik and Edward Gura, as security personnel to a convoy of over one hundred lorries. We were to escort them through the northern part of the Sinai desert through Palestine, Syria, Iraq, to Persia, north of Tehran, where the R.A.F. had a large base. On the outskirts of this airfield, the Polish army had organised a transit camp for the refugees arriving from the southern part of Russia after Stalin had released them. There must have been hundreds of thousands of these people in the camp, living in tents provided by Britain and America. The conditions they were living in were the best that could be provided, considering the difficulties of the time.

During the two days following our arrival, the Commanding Officer of the transit camp had sorted out the families who were to go, and made them ready. Early the following morning, at sunrise, the convoy assembled in a long line, one of my colleagues, Henryk, being in the first vehicle. Edward was in the middle, and I followed at the end. Each of us was equipped with a shortwave radio transmitter.

Within two hours of our departure from the transit camp, I began to learn that our guard duty would not be the easy post I had imagined. Suddenly, the convoy came to a halt to provide people the chance to relieve themselves; there were, of course, no toilets on the trucks. None of us three policemen had any experience with convoys before, and getting the people on and off was not easy; they wanted a longer rest. We laid down, however, that there to be only ten minute stops every two hours for this purpose.

Our first stop was Baghdad, where we spent the night in a transit camp already provided for the refugees, where they were supplied with a hot meal from the field kitchens, facilities for showers, and emergency clothing for those who needed it. At daybreak the following morning we started the convoy on it's journey again, heading for Palestine. We finally reached Gaza, the journey being quite peaceful and easy, except for the people who had just come from a cold country, and for whom the heat was torture. Many elderly people just collapsed and needed medical attention. Fortunately, thanks to the good organisation of the Polish forces, we had three ambulances with the convoy and medical supplies were plentiful. If the ambulances had to halt to attend to them, I stayed behind, since it was my responsibility to see to it that no vehicles in the convoy fell behind me.

When we reached Cairo, I noticed that none of the people in the convoy expressed any surprise at their surroundings, even when they saw the pyramids or the Sphinx. Their emotions seemed to have left them through the hardship of the 1939 campaign, and having been made to work like slaves in Russian farms and factories.

We stayed outside Cairo for about ten days, where everyone was interrogated prior to being issued with identity papers. They were also all issued with new clothing and given a certain amount of money for their personal use. We security men had a few days rest during this time, as the people at the transit camp were responsible for the safety of our charges. After all this had been done, the convoy moved on, going south, to cross the Sahara desert. There were no roads, just tracks, and in some cases, even they had been covered by sand during sandstorms, and therefore the compass was our chief guide. There was only one map, which was with Henryk, who guided the convoy from the front. When we left Cairo, we had been given four trucks loaded with food, and a water tanker, so that we could stop at night wherever we were - there was no need to look for an oasis.

The heat was a perpetual problem, especially as we came nearer and nearer to the Equator. There were a number of casualties; the severe heat was a killer, and we buried between seventy and eighty elderly people on the journey.

Driving was hot and boring, and it was difficult keeping awake. In fact, once I fell asleep! I had been driving as the rearguard of the convoy. I was awakened by a terrific jolt, to find my jeep stuck with it's front wheels over a steep cliff. Another moment, and I would have been over the edge. As it was, I managed to lock the jeep's wheels and then reverse, and pull back - not a nice moment.

After that I followed my tracks back until I picked up the wheel tracks of the convoy, and just followed them till I found them where they had camped for the night. Nobody had missed me, so it was as well for me that I was able to get myself out of trouble. Actually, so many other drivers had similar experiences that it became a rule that the rear driver had to have somebody with him from the convoy to see that he kept awake.

On the other side of the Sahara there were other dangers. When you got into the forests, or were crossing the mountains, the local Africans kept an eye on the convoys. There were instances of them attacking to rob and kill. Sometimes, women who went for a pee behind the nearest bushes did not come back - they disappeared, to be raped, robbed or eaten, or maybe all three, because the tribesmen there were really a primitive lot, with personal habits which were completely indescribable. This meant the women had to take security guards with them into the bushes when they did their business - trouble is, they did not realise the danger, and preferred to risk being eaten!

If they disappeared on the journey, there was no record of them, they just disappeared, since when they left Russia they were allocated numbers, and their names and other details were not recorded till they reached Salisbury - they would just vanish.

The journey down to Salisbury took about seven days and eight nights. Twenty miles south of the city was a large Polish camp with tents and quite comfortable sleeping facilities. At this stage, the camp was well organised, they formed their own community and their own local governing body with security guards who performed police duties, schools and hospitals provided by the Polish forces. The whole place was set up on a semi-permanent basis, and many people lived there till 1948, after which most of them moved to Great Britain, where the majority still are. I went on convoys like this eight times after I joined the military police.

One thing I found hard to find was a girlfriend, in spite of all these Polish people being there for me to search among. There were not many young ladies around - Stalin tended to 'export' only the older people where he could. Also, for obvious reasons, the prisoners-of-war he sent back tended to be male. And those women who were there tended to be rather selective. In fact, I only went out with one Polish girl. One reason was that such girls as were around always wanted officers, and so when they went to dances, they would feel your epaulette in the dim light of the dance floor to find out what rank you were.

Another reason was that, in Polish society, rules relating to sex, love and marriage were very strict, and this attitude ruled in the military as well - if you wanted to have a woman, you had to go to the next town, where you were not known, and in different uniform.

Although I had been selected for the secret service, I did not just lay around between missions - nor did I receive any extra pay for this dangerous duty, just the normal soldier's pay. And, as I have just shown, I did ordinary police duty, which was totally separate from my 'secret life.'

One of my worst experiences while in the military police, as distinct to being on my missions, happened in Ancona, about mid-August, 1944. (This was after the invasion of Italy.) I had just come back from my third mission, and could have done with a rest. Instead, I found myself right in the middle of a terrific fight.

At Ancona, there was a place which reminded me of Gibraltar - a high rock with a fortress inside. There is a port there too, on north west side of the town.

The High Command had learned a lesson from Monte Cassino, where they had lost so many men to so little purpose - it was a dreadful mistake, no matter what the history books may say. They decided to use deception to achieve their ends.

I was on traffic control that day from about 2pm, just outside the town. There were many tanks moving about in the fields, mostly moving up to the brow of the hill from which you could see Ancona. After two hours, at about 4pm, a number of tank transporters came along, and took aboard nearly all the best tanks, leaving only four or five, old British tanks from the desert. These dragged trees around the fields to cause dust so that, from a distance, it looked as if there were many tanks still there.

The Germans shelled the hill, but to no purpose. None of the tanks were hit. And by the time they had really got going, I was stationed on the top of another hill, and was in no danger, just watching the show. When night fell, the tanks were still roaring their engines, and moving about slowly, here and there, keeping up the deception.

That night, at 0400 hours, came the general alarm, and everyone went to battle stations. In fact, what had happened was that the tank transporters had come and moved the bulk of the tanks forward five kilometres past Ancona, to the northern outskirts of the town, and had cut the German lines of communication, isolating it. We all went forward, and I went with them, to establish traffic control just behind the front line. We really took the Germans by surprise, and I saw German officers in their pyjamas firing their Schmeissers at our troops. Ancona surrendered at about 0500 or 0600 hours, and they were not even able to blow up the fortress, for the sappers de-fused their mine.

At midday the following day, I was on traffic control at a big road island at a roundabout at the bottom of the hill; right outside the Port of Ancona, on the right is the town of Ancona, and to the left is the main road to Senegalia, Pesaro and Rimini and to the south the main road from Porto St. Georgio, on which road our part of the Polish forces had been in action before the capture of Ancona. There is a big road island here, where traffic control posts were always maintained while allied troops were in the area. On the East side of the town, there was a rock like hill. The fortifications there, as I have said, reminded me of Gibraltar. The Italians had constructed a fortress inside the rock, and the Germans had expanded it and placed heavy guns inside for firing on ships.

On this particular day I had just finished my early morning traffic control duty, which had started at 0600 hours and finished at 1400 hours around the road island at Ancona, which I have just described. After coming off duty, I was driving my jeep back towards HQ at Porto St. Georgio. Half way up the hill was the most enormous explosion, and my jeep was lifted into the air; for a moment I thought I had hit a land mine. As I recovered myself, I turned my eyes back towards Ancona, only to find that the roundabout and the road island were no longer there. The Germans had apparently set up a timed explosion, with five tons of explosive.

Not a trace of one living soul was to be seen. Everyone in the vicinity of the explosion had been killed; the buildings had been demolished. The dead included my own colleague, to whom I had handed over. So enormous were the effects of the explosion that they reached as far as the harbour, where a small boat was sunk as a result.

Life as a military policeman was certainly not without incidents and problems. On one occasion, a report reached our Headquarters that a few hundred tyres had disappeared at one of our spares stores at a transport depot. However, no official report or complaint had come from the officer in charge. To eliminate any queries or doubts about the situation, my commanding officers had instructed my colleague Jan Jazemski and I to investigate the matter.

The depot was outside Lorreto, which was located on top of a hill, and it occupied about a square mile - a large place. When we arrived, we went directly to the commanding officer. He greeted us with a smile: "What can we do for you gentlemen?" My colleague replied with a question, "Do you have any problems here, like robberies, attacks, or any materials missing?"

The commanding officer replied: "In fact, we do have a small problem, and I have already organised an investigation into it. There are several tyres of various sizes missing, and I have interrogated all the soldiers in the depot, and some admitted to small offences, involving stealing a few spare parts and trading them for wine and other delicacies or giving them to their girlfriends' relatives. All offenders who admitted to such offences have been severely punished, as is written in the record." He then handed us a few sheets of typed paper which confirmed his explanation. "However," he continued, "the problem I have got is on a slightly larger scale, as tyres keep disappearing and we can never find how they disappear from the camp."

My friend and I inspected the whole depot area and we found no leak in the security system. We decided to report as such to our HQ. After leaving the depot, we came to a place where there were a few olive trees next to the road, and I suggested to my colleague that we ought to have a break and a snack, to which he agreed. We parked the jeep at the side of the road and sat under the olive trees eating and drinking; including a bottle of wine. And as I was eating, I was looking right across the valley, admiring the view and the village at the bottom of the hill.

Suddenly, I saw a tyre rolling down the hill towards the village - for a moment, I could not trust my sight. I waited, and there came another.

I nudged my colleague, and said: "Look at that, what do you think?" and sure enough, he could see it too. Without waiting to finish our snack, we got up and removed our caps, so that we would not be recognised as military police. My colleague then walked down the valley to the village, and I drove the mile and a half back to the depot.

When I arrived, the Commanding Officer was talking to his men; when he saw me, he dismissed them and came towards me. Before he managed to ask any questions, I jumped out of the jeep and asked him to follow me; I also asked him to order some soldiers to surround the area, but to proceed with caution and in utmost silence. This he did, and once we had encircled the area, we found three boys aged between eight and nine. One was holding the barbed wire apart, and the other two were taking the tyres and rolling them downhill towards the village; of course, once they were in motion, gravity did the rest.

We arrested all three boys and took them to the Commanding Cfficer. From his office he telephoned the carabinieri, the Italian police, and I telephoned my HQ for help, since we needed more help to search the village. After the help arrived, we proceeded with the Commanding Officer to the village, which was called Lorretano.

In the centre of the village there was a small square, with a well and a water trough. After an intensive search through the village, which lasted over two hours, all we found was one tyre lying between the olive trees just outside the village. Yet my colleague and I had seen more than one tyre rolling down the hill. There had to be more tyres somewhere; but we could not find them.

When the search was called off, one or two of the men were thirsty and I suggested a drink of cool water from the well; there was a wooden bucket attached to the end of the rope, with the usual crank handle. After I tugged, and found that the bucket felt full, my colleague started cranking it up and after a few turns found the crank would not move any further. I got hold of the rope and started shaking it, thinking the bucket had got stuck on the wall of the well somewhere.

Then I glanced into the well, and for the second time that day I could hardly believe what I saw. The whole well was lined with tyres, and the bucket was running inside the ring of tyres, on one of which it had stuck. Our thirst had solved the Commanding Officer's problem. The Civil Authority then took action, and several people were prosecuted for their actions; though I imagine the boys escaped with a telling off; one cannot do much to children of that age.

That was one of the more light-hearted incidents. Another, which I can remember well, involved no danger for me, but was sobering and distressing. I had received an order to despatch a secret message up close to the battle line, near Faenza. I used a motorbike for this journey (I had learned to ride properly by now), and I arrived about ten o'clock in the evening. After identifying myself to the guard, he pointed out the Commanding Officer's tent to me. As I neared the tent, I heard what I thought was a low crying noise; however, I could not be sure, because there was artillery fire going on not far off, and it was difficult to be sure I heard anything. I dismissed the matter from my mind, and tried to knock on the tent's supporting post; but there was no answer. I entered; the tent was lit by a portable gas lamp.

By the field table, there was a British officer, with his head on his hands, whispering to himself; "...all these men have died for nothing..." he kept repeating, and then he asked himself, over and over again, "Why did I do it? Why did I do it?" He also said other things which I could not understand, partly due to my lack of English, and partly because he spoke so low.

I did not wish him to realise that I had seen him, since it would embarrass him, so I stepped back out of the tent, and called in a loud voice: "Is anybody there?" Seconds later, a voice said: "Come in." When I entered, he was sitting up straight, and after saluting him, I said, "I have brought you an urgent despatch, which is classified." He opened it, asked me to step outside and wait. After a few minutes, he came out and told me there was no reply. I returned to my HQ. I am sure that similar guilt must have affected many Commanding Officers in such a way; command is always a lonely business, and such people suffer the more because they can never show any weakness. I knew that from my time commanding groups in the partisans. One must always be confident, or your troops lose confidence. Each commander has his own lonely journey to tread.

So, even when I was 'safe' behind our lines, there were dangers and sometimes horrible experiences to cope with. But for all that, the strain and terror I endured on my 'secret' missions were far worse. I never knew when these missions would come. I would just be summoned, and be given my marching orders. Since my first mission had gone well, they were always on the look out for work for me. So now I shall talk about my second and third missions, which were both uniquely terrible in their own ways.

Chapter 18

THE SECOND MISSION

We were outside Foggia at the time, on the East coast of Italy, and the Allied front must have been up near Rome. The battle moved towards the southern side of Foggia in the late afternoon. There was a very high bridge down at the bottom of a canyon, crossing the river. A few hundred Polish infantrymen crossed the bridge to the Northern side of the river, but because of sunset, and the resultant lack of air support, they were ordered to withdraw back over the bridge to the south. The commanders knew that the Germans had mined the bridge across the river - but it was thought that they had not had time to make the final connections to make the mines 'live.' They were right, but during the night the Germans made those final connections. As a consequence, when the tanks were ordered to cross the bridge the next morning, thinking that it was still safe, they were blown up high with the bridge. I shall never forget seeing those tanks fall like toys from the bridge to the river about a hundred and fifty feet below.

That was the beginning of the battle of Foggia. It was in fact, one of the biggest battles in the East coast of Italy fought by the Polish forces, ranking only after Cassino. On the second day of the battle, I was suddenly recalled to the Intelligence HQ, which was now located in Sicily, in the city of Catania, where I went directly to report to the Commanding Officer. I was flown in a small plane from outside Brindisi straight to Catania. During the journey, I had already calculated that I was going to be asked to go on another mission. When I arrived, the commanding officer got up and came to meet me, smiling broadly, and with his arms stretched out, very friendly and informal, saying "How nice to see you again!"

I smiled in return, shaking his hand, saying, "Where is it this time?" To which he answered, "All in good time, one cannot discuss this matter on an empty stomach." Walking to his cocktail cabinet he poured out two glasses of vodka. Then, turning to me, he handed me a glass, he lifted his glass to mine- and said: "To our next success," then continued in a quiet voice, "It is much simpler than the last one."

Believing what he said, I relaxed; however, in my heart of hearts I knew he was lying. After finishing our drinks, he turned to me and said: "Now for the food," and his driver, who was already waiting outside, stood to attention as we left and opened the doors of his car as we approached. We went to the best hotel, which was much frequented by the Americans, who had money to spend. After sitting down, he started to quietly explain to me what he had in mind for my next mission.

He stressed that the job was quite simple, just to eliminate a female double-agent from whom we had no information of late, and whom we had learned from another source co-operated a lot with the Gestapo. "The mission will not take two or three days," he went on, "and you will be returning in the same uniform as you leave in - that is, as far as the Italian border, and I am sure you will then know your way back here. The only difference will be that once back in Italy, you should contact partisan HQ in either Florence or Milan and transmit a message that you will receive later on. We will arrange for a motor boat to pick you up somewhere near Ravenna. The partisan HQ will inform you of the details and guide you to the pick-up point."

During this conversation, we were having a wonderful meal and had drunk a few glasses of vodka. In conclusion, he informed me that I would be staying at headquarters to await my departure. He wanted me to meet a Polish colleague of mine who would be joining me in the journey to Germany, though he had a separate job to do, nothing to do with my mission.

After arrival at HQ, I was guided by the batman (whom I had met before) to my quarters and I decided to take as much rest as I could while still in safe surroundings. The next day, I reported to the commanding officer for further instructions, and was handed a thick envelope with all the details of my mission, including the maps of the 'drop zone' and the name and addresses of my intended victim, which I had to memorise before leaving. That afternoon, I met another Polish officer, Josph Sikora, who spoke fluent German; I knew him, we had been in training together, but this was his first mission.

He questioned me about the kind of behaviour he could expect from the German people he might meet, and how he should behave. I told him, very simply, that he need not worry. He would be dressed as a German officer, and therefore need not worry about the German people; only about other officers, since everyone else would automatically obey him and be afraid of him; which, of course, was the reason we were given officers' identities. It automatically protected us from the scrutiny of 95% of the people we would meet; he would be in charge, and must act accordingly, confidently and arrogantly. We had quite a general discussion, but did not discuss the nature of our individual missions. Before we realised how quickly the time had gone, there was a knock on the door, and there was the Commanding Officer, saying: "I am so pleased that you two are getting on well together, because this will help both of you make a successful mission." Then he went on: "I suggest that both of you have a good rest tonight and try to converse as much as you can in German tomorrow morning. Perfect yourself and imagine yourself in the surroundings you will be in shortly."

With these words he baded us goodnight, and walked away. Minutes later, my colleague said "Goodnight" to me and I went to bed. After turning the lights off I must have laid in bed for about two hours imagining in my mind the new territory I was about to explore and the people I was shortly going to meet. With these thoughts in mind, I fell into a deep sleep. The following day, about eleven o'clock in the morning, we received an order to report to the Commanding Officer. After we did so, he asked if we had memorised all the information we had been told about. After we had assured him that we had, he instructed us to go and follow the batman to another room where the German uniforms were waiting for us. As Josph was about to wear a German uniform for the first time, the batman had to attend mostly to him, whilst I saw to myself. During this performance we had a good laugh at each other, mostly trying to remember in which battle we received our numerous decorations. I had no problem with this, since the uniform was the one I had worn previously, and my identity papers were the same too; I was once more Major Hoffman, the hero of the Russian front. Josph became Major Kupper. After dressing, the batman told us to stay in the room till departure, which would be at 1900 hours. In the meantime, he suggested we go through our papers once more.

After lunch, the Commanding Officer came in and discussed my mission in detail in one corner of the room, while 'Major Kupper' sat in another corner looking through his own orders. I was told that both of us would travel on the same plane, an American Super Fortress. I felt very uneasy on hearing this, as we knew very well that a lot of Super Fortresses had been shot down during raids. The Commanding Officer explained that only one Super Fortress would be flying tonight, with us on board, and it was likely that the German anti-aircraft guns would not bother to fire, preferring to conceal their positions till a real raid; a situation which was usual - they did not usually bother with lone planes. I was then asked to leave while 'Major Kupper' received a more detailed briefing, since this was his first mission and he needed the extra help. Obviously, I did not need to know this information, and therefore was not told it, as is usual in security work, for what you do not know, you cannot tell, no matter what the circumstances.

All afternoon we concentrated on making sure that we understood everything to do with our missions, so that we could act without hesitation - often an essential if you are to succeed. At 1700 hours, an HQ car took us to near Palermo, to the airfield, which was crowded with Super Fortresses and the driver, previously informed of which plane was ours, took us straight to it. We boarded at once, and (unlike the position on my first mission) we were sitting over the bomb doors, which had a quarter inch gap in them right under our feet. This alarmed me, and I insisted on a parachute before take off, having little faith in American pilots or their crew; the thought in my mind was that they could pull the wrong lever and tip me out of the bomb doors. I also made sure my parachute was tied to the hitching bar, and 'Major Kupper' took the same precaution; that ensured that if the worst happened, our parachutes would open automatically.

Shortly afterwards, we took off, and proceeded over the sea towards Germany. Our 'drop zone' was located between Hamburg and Bremen, slightly to the south west of Hamburg. During our flight, 'Major Kupper' became very nervous and on one or two occasions tried to talk to me in Polish; however, I just smiled and replied in German, warning him that this was the biggest mistake, and his life depended on avoiding such mistakes. Soon after 23.30 hours, we were told that we would reach the 'drop zone' in one minute, and were also told to take hold of the side struts of the aircraft and wait until the doors were completely opened. I arranged with 'Major Kupper' that since I was on my second mission, I dropped first, and that he should follow me on a count of three. When the signal was given by one of the crew, I released my hold and floated through the air, watching the parachute open. Seconds later, I saw my colleague following me.

As we landed, we removed our parachute harness, and rolled the parachutes up together, and ran in a westerly direction to nearby bushes where we stayed for half an hour until we heard a car engine. The car stopped on the road, not far away. A woman in a German uniform got out, pretending she needed to answer a 'call of nature'. As she passed us, she spoke the codeword quietly; repeating it twice, pausing and repeating it again. I replied in a similar manner, and we emerged from the bushes and went with her to the car, a beautiful civilian Mercedes. As we started off, she said: "I am Margarita, Margarita Krupper."

The name suddenly had me on guard; that was the name of the person I had come to eliminate. I did not expect her to drive us in the right direction, since I knew she no longer supplied us with information, and was probably treacherous. Of course we had been briefed on where we should be taken, and as a precaution I asked her to stop and sat in the front seat, next to her. I was very tense, and kept a strict check on the direction in which we were heading. We encountered a German Military Police checkpoint, and passed it successfully; after which I ordered her to sit in the passenger seat, while I drove. I imagined that by then my tension would have made her realise she was not trusted. 'Major Kupper' and I did not exchange a single word, but I heard later that he was surprised at my action.

After driving for about forty minutes, we reached our appointed destination and I asked her sharply which house we were to report to. She hesitated, then pointed it out. It was a large building, and I knew the occupants were our friends, and therefore, after entering the house and exchanging the recognition code, we began to relax. Nevertheless, I kept a very sharp eye on Margarita. It had been dark during the drive, and now that I could see her properly in the light I could see that she was a very beautiful young woman, possibly a year or two older than I, and if it had not been for the war, I could have fallen in love with her on first sight.

At about 0200 hours one of the occupants of the 'safe house' told 'Major Kupper' that his car had arrived and that the driver was a very trusted person and knew his destination precisely and would give him his final instructions, and also arrange for his return journey. Off he went, while I stayed and spent the rest of the night talking to Margarita. I had begun to feel more soft towards her, for she reminded me very much of a young girl who used to live next door whilst I was living in Chyrow. She had naturally curly blonde hair, beautiful blue eyes and a face like a little girl; she was about five feet six inches tall, with a beautiful figure. Well, I am as susceptible to female charm as the next man. I was supposed to kill her immediately, but I decided to disobey orders, and give her a chance.

The following morning, Margarita told me that she had to go to the office where she worked. She saw I was nervous, and assured me that I had nothing to worry about; that she would not betray me and that she would return in the late afternoon to see me again. And off she went. It sounds ridiculous now - being assured by someone with whom you were on perfecctly friendly terms that you would not betray them. Yet one was always nervous of just that. Even if the person seeemed trustworthy you were worried that they might make some mistake. In her case, of course, I was worried that she might be working for the other side - but naturally I could not tell her that.

She arrived back between four ad five o'clock in the afternoon, and gave me a very friendly kiss. Before I managed to say a word she informed me that she was going to have next two days off and we could go to the countryside to spend two days together, providing I had nothing else urgent to do. I said: "Most certainly. I am entitled to have a rest occasionally." (She was of course under the impression that I had come to do some job that was nothing to do with her, and she never questioned me about it. Knowing that I would say nothing in any case.) She told me that it would be of benefit to my work to get to know the surrounding area well - an excuse for being able to get me away, of course, out in the circumstances. I was happy to go along with it.

She told our agents in the building what she proposed to do. I still had doubts about her and her plans, but was still ready to give her a chance. Minutes later, our agent gave me a suitcase with spare clothing and' we joined Margarita and walked to the waiting car. Margarita drove, and after a half hour's journey we arrived at a large old country cottage outside Hamburg. It was completely isolated and the nearest house was four and a half miles away. There was an elderly German woman in charge there, and as we were introduced Margarita put a hand to her mouth behind the woman's back. I knew this meant that I had to be careful what I said - the elderly woman was not 'one of us'. I just nodded in reply to let her know that I understood.

We went updstairs to the bedroom, which was a converted attic, and I could see at once by the tasteful way it was laid out that it had had the benefit of the 'woman's touch.' I stood speechless - being invited to this very feminine bedroom seemed an open sexual invitiation. Normally speaking I would have been very pleased and settled in - but I was in a very difficult situation. However, Margarita did not bother about my qualms - after all, she did not know about half of them! She went to the dressing table, saying, "Are you going to stand there all night?" Then,

seeing the stupid expression on my face, she continued:
"I hope you have nothing against me because I like you very much and
it is not my habit to bring any man here whom I do not like."

Her reaction was so straightforward and natural that I felt easier in
my heart, and more affectionate towards her. I stepped forward and
started unpacking my clothes. She pointed out a fitted wardrobe and
said I could use it whilst I was here. Then she pointed to the opposite
side of the bedroom and indicated the bathroom, and told me that
dinner would be served in an hour. I was unpacking my clothes and did
not notice what Margarita was doing; when I turned round I found that
she was standing there in her underwear. I had a strange feeling. I had
come here under orders to kill her, and here we were, behaving as
lovers. My nervousness made me behave strangely. I said: "Excuse
me, I'll go and have a shower." And off I walked towards the
bathroom, still in my uniform. She laughed and said: "You're not
going to have a shower in your uniform, are you?"

"I'll undress in the bathroom," said I.

"Don't be silly," she said, "You get undressed here, you must start
to feel at home here." She thought the whole thing was just caused by
my shyness. I had never had any experience like this before, and
eventually I took my uniform off and just left my underwear on and
went to have my shower. When I returned to the bedroom, she was
already dressed for dinner, and said: "If I were you, I would put your
best uniform on, because the housekeeper will think there is
something wrong with an officer if he is not properly dressed for
dinner."

After our meal, and in the presence of the housekeeper, she
suggested we ought to go and have a rest in the bedroom! She even
said: "I am going to have a hard day tomorrow, therefore I need plenty
of rest." I was still a very simple boy in many ways, in spite of my
experiences, and I took her speech very seriously. When I got to the
bedroom, I really thought we were going to rest! Needless to say, we
did not get much - in fact we did not get to sleep till well after midnight
- but the time went very pleasantly for all that.

My dilemma continued. I could not believe and accept that a woman
with Margarita's capacity for fun and affection was a double agent. She
seemed to have a definite leaning towards democracy and against
Nazism. For my part, I did not mention politics too much - that would
have been too dangerous. But I did make a number of remarks which
indicated that Nazism really had no place in a modern, democratic

state. These remarks went down all right - but then, she was in love with me. I was still unsure and puzzled.

The following morning, she kissed me au revoir, telling me that she was going to do some shopping in the local shopping centre and would be back within two hours. I sat about and amused myself as best I could, and sure enough she was as good as her word, and returned as she said she would - a big relief, since I was still half expecting the Gestapo to turn up. We went off in one of the cars (she had two - she was obviously privileged) and went for a drive in the country where we spent most of the time playing, almost like children. In the evening, we came home and the events of the previous evening and night repeated themselves.

The following day was a copy of the one before. However, after dinner she informed me that she had to go to her cousin, who lived south of Hamburg. He was called Krugger, and was a Colonel in the SS; if she did not show up, he would start a search for her. I thought it over, and decided to accompany her.

After a short journey, we arrived at a large mansion in the countryside, and she told me that this belonged to her late uncle, who had been killed during a bombing raid on Hamburg. Her cousin, Colonel Krugger, lived there now and he ran his office in the mansion with some of his staff; he was in charge of security at a machine-gun factory. I told her that as long as she played our game, no harm would come to her, and she promised to be faithful. She then introduced me to her cousin, and he seemed delighted to meet me; of course he only knew me as Major Hoffman, a distinguished officer from the Russian front; and he admired my decorations. He said that he needed Margarita's services urgently, and suggested that we both stay in the mansion for a few days. I did not like this; firstly because I wanted her company, being half in love with her by that time, and secondly because I still did not quite trust her, and wanted to keep her under my eye. However, I could hardly do anything but give in; to do otherwise would have inevitably meant raising suspicions. I was completely torn between love and suspicion; though after we were left alone she renewed her promise not to betray me.

Most of the day we went round talking to various officers, and she was by my side most of the time. We got to know each other better and better, and towards the evening, before we started back to the mansion (we had been at the factory during the day) she gave me a kiss on the cheek. I said: "Surely you can do better than that?" (Yes, I was getting over my shyness with women by that time!) and she answered: "I have not had much experience up to now, but I find you extremely pleasant company, so therefore I might as well try it," and before I realised what was happening I received a very passionate kiss, more passionate than any I had received to date.

Back at the mansion, we were informed by the butler that dinner would be served in half an hour. When everything was ready, we were asked to join Colonel Krugger in his study for a drink before dinner. I met Margarita on the first floor landing with a big smile and a kiss on the cheek. We walked together donw the stairway into the main hallway hand in hand. She was very cheerful, she whispered to me quietly, "Ich liebe dich - I love you," to which I replied, rather lamely, "Danke - thanks." At this point, we spotted Major Karl Krugger entering the hall from his study. Seeing us, he smiled and said: "Already lovers?" to which she replied: "Just good friends. After all, who can resist the Iron Cross?" (The Iron Cross was among the decorations I wore.)

He invited us, very politely, to have a drink. We had two glasses of champagne each, then went to the dining hall, which had a very long table with about forty to fifty chairs round it. We were alone, and Karl sat at the top of the table, with Margarita on his right hand and I on his left. During the meal, we gossiped about simple matters, all nothing to do with the war, and towards the end of the meal, he turned to me, and suggested that afterwards I should tell him more about the Russian front, as the farthest he had ever been into Russia had been Vinnica, and therefore he would like to know more about the surroundings of Stalingrad, which was were I was supposed to have been in action. I grew rather nervous, for of course I knew nothing about Stalingrad.

After dinner, we went into the lounge, and Karl told the butler to bring two bottles of champagne; I was talking to Margarita, but what Karl said attracted my attention, for he mentioned a champagne I had never heard of, and when I asked from what country it came, he said, "Oh, it is our special champagne," and, turning to the butler, said, "You know, the special one that we always have for our guests." Somehow, I did not like the sound of this; I can only think that I picked up some undertone in his voice, for one's senses become unusually sharp when one is in danger. The butler left, and Karl began walking around the hall talking about the pictures on the wall.

Then the butler returned with three glasses already filled with champagne; each of us reached for a glass, but I saw something in

Karl's eyes which put me even more on guard. As Margarita reached for her glass, he watched her closely, and me also. She drank all the champagne, but I pretended to sip and never touched a drop. At this point, I saw that Karl kept his glass close to his mouth, but showed no sign of drinking it. I still was half-thinking that I was imagining things, and started to converse with Karl; but then I noticed that Margarita was swaying on her feet. Karl turned to me, saying, "Come on, let's drink to your next brave and successful action."

I pretended not to hear what he said, and watched Margarita. Suddenly she dropped the glass and began to fall backwards. I dropped my glass and jumped to catch her. Karl was standing at my left hand, saying that she had probably had one too many, but her face gave a different impression; she was paralysed or dying. I knew she had been happy and in good form before the meal, and was sure that this was not illness, but something much worse.

I was now glacially calm; I was on one knee by Margarita's body, checking her pulse at her neck and wrists. But my experiences had taught me to be very wary, and even as I checked that Margarita was indeed dead, I kept one corner of my eye on Karl. Suddenly I realised his gun holster was open and his right hand was twitching; I did not hesitate. I moved my right hand, unseen by him, and pulled out my Luger. As I turned, my gun pointed at his head, and he drew his gun in turn and fired. Fortunately he was a bad shot, and missed my head by a small margin. Thanks to my experience with the partisans, my aim was better, and my bullet caught him in the centre of the forehead.

I knew now I was back in action; leaving the two dead bodies where they lay, I moved rapidly, knowing that swift action alone could save me. Someone would have heard the shot; the butler if nobody else. I ran to the door, and found three cars parked in front of the house. I jumped into the first, a Mercedes, and luckily found the ignition key in place. I started it, and drove away at top speed, already thinking about my escape; in my pocket I held a forged priority travel order prepared against just this emergency, which said that I was urgently needed at the Italian front; an order which had been given to me by the agents in the 'safe house' in Hamburg.

At Dusseldorf station, I reported to the military commandant of the station, and handed over these orders. He pointed out a goods train with two passenger coaches tacked onto the end, and told me that this train was going direct to Florence, and that the commandant of the train was a Major Glantt, and that I might be of assistance to him if by any chance I spoke Russian or Polish. The train was conveying Russian and Polish labourers to Italy to help construct concrete bunkers around Florence, and Major Glantt had nobody with any knowledge of these languages, and the train had to leave at once.

This sounded like a good chance for me, and I immediately crossed several railway lines to the waiting train. Major Glantt was not there, however his adjutant, a Lieutenant, was; I presented my orders to him, and he said that he was sure Major Glantt would not mind having another officer for company, as there was a spare compartment, so I would not be in the way. As we were speaking, the train started to move, and soon after, Major Glantt came in from the platform of the goods wagon. Seeing me, he said, "I see we have company." I saluted him, and said "Heil Hitler." He smiled, came towards me with a laugh, and said: "What is your pleasure?" His adjutant handed him my papers, which he studied with great interest, and then said: "That's quite in order. As you have been at the Russian front, can I ask if you have any knowledge of Russian or Polish?"

I replied: "It so happens that I learnt Russian whilst I was in Russia, and some Polish too, from the people in a labour camp."

"That is very useful, because none of our men speak either of those languages. You will be very helpful if you would not mind interpreting and sorting out any problems which I have with the labourers during the journey." He also told me that because the labourers were needed so urgently, there would only be six stops, and solely to change engines. He had made himself comfortable on the train, and had a butler with him! This man came in and announced that a meal would be ready in a few minutes.

Shortly after dinner, the train came to a halt in Frankfurt, where the engines were changed, and a few minutes later we were on our way towards Strasbourg. In Strasbourg, the people from the labour camp left the train and were served from a field kitchen with a hot meal and allowed to use the toilet facilities. My knowledge of their languages proved very useful, and I conversed with a number of them and sorted out minor problems. Major Glantt was very pleased with my help, and after we had started the next stage of the journey brought out a bottle of Schnapps, and his two lieutenants joined myself and him in a drink, wishing each other success in the near future.

Naturally, socialising like this with the enemy was a rather difficult business, and I could not drink too much; in the end I excused myself, and said I needed rest before I returned to my duties on the southern front. As I lay in bed, I heard my companions referring to me jokingly as the Schlafen Major. However, I did not sleep; I am always cautious, and did not wish to let my guard down for a minute. About three hours later the adjutant knocked on the door, and enquired if I was awake, as Major Glantt would like to speak to me. I told him I would only be a few moments; when I came into the mobile office Glantt occupied, I found him looking very worried and holding some papers.

"Here I am," he said, "with two officers and sixteen men to escort the train on this long journey, and I have begun to worry that some of the men might try to desert, especially when we cross the Alps and are in Italy." By this time we were nearing Lyons in Southern France, where, once more, the men were given a hot meal and supplied with fresh water. The Major got more concerned as the journey continued; and obviously wanted my help and advice. It was difficult to know what to say; he had fifteen hundred men to supervise, and the escort was indeed very small, and his fears were probably well founded. I sympathised and played my part of helpful fellow officer.

A few hours later, we passed Torino in Italy, where the steam engine was replaced by an electric one and we proceeded to Bologna. This was our last stop, for a German army transport train had priority over ours. With that steaming ahead of us, we arrived in Florence at 1600 hours. I was about to say goodbye to Major Glantt, when that worried man asked me if I could assist him in explaining to the men what their next job and destination was to be. Still keeping up my helpful role, I agreed. It was rather bizarre, but of course I was the only one to understand the joke. I faced about fifteen hundred men of various nationalities, just such a gang as I had served in under Herr Terjung, and most of whom understood Polish or Russian, and told them to wait for the German or Italian road transport which would take them to where they would begin their construction work. There were several questions about where they were going. I knew, but said: "Wait and see, you'll find out."

Then I said goodbye to Major Glantt, and vanished as quickly as I could. Of course I knew Florence reasonably well, and found the Albergo Nationale, where I chatted with the waiter. Then I went round the shops and bought myself some civilian clothes, and, sensing I could trust the shopkeeper, asked him for a room in which to change, and did so in his presence. He asked me if I was deserting from the German forces, since, if that was the case, he could possibly help me. I thanked him, but left it at that, since he was rather cautious, and told him that I knew my way from there. I also asked him to hide the uniform or destroy it. As I walked away, I noted his telephone number and then went directly to the partisan HQ in Florence.

I identified myself, and they provided me with transport to Ravenna, where I met another guide who escorted me to the torpedo boat which would take me back to Sicily. All went well; I returned after precisely three weeks, and on my arrival at Catania was greeted by my Commanding Officer with another great big smile and a couple of glasses of vodka. I reported that my mission was successfully concluded; though some of the details, as you may guess, I kept to myself. He told me that my colleague Josph had successfully completed his' mission also, and was now on his way back to headquarters under the protection of the Italian partisans.

It was rather embarrassing to report my affair with Margarita, the woman I was sent to kill! (After a good deal of thought, I decided that the best course was to tell the entire and complete truth.) However, his only reaction was to say: "Lucky you!" and tease me about the whole incident! I suppose that from his point of view Margarita was dead, guilty or not, and there was no point in making a fuss about it.

Of course, there were still mysteries about the whole affair which I never solved - they were just permanent loose ends. Why did Krugger poison myself and Margarita? For of course he must have intended to kill both of us. His action in not drinking showed that all three glasses of champagne were poisoned - from the rapidity of Margarita's death, I expect he used cyanide - there are few other poisons that work so fast. I can only think that he suspected Margarita of being a double agent, and decided that since I was obviously involved with her, he would wipe us both out to make sure. But why did he not inform the local Gestapo? My guess is that he feared that he would find a black mark on his record, or worse. Maybe, even, he had sold information to Margarita, and had later regretted his treachery, yet feared that it might be discovered. Or perhaps Margarita had been stealing information from his office, and he had found out - and wished to end the leak without a trace on his security record. Who knows? In the murky world of a spy, there are dead ends and unexplained mysteries all the time. Certainly, as far as I was concerned, I did not even know of Krugger's existence before Margarita introduced us - as far as I was concerned, the whole thing was inexplicable. Perhaps, somewhere, some individual, maybe an aging German intelligence officer, knows the answer - if they read this, I would like to unravel the mystery at last.

After that, I got a week's leave, and then, with four other military policemen, went back to normal duty as a security man on a naval convoy. From Catania, in a half empty troop ship, I travelled to Port Said, where I changed ships and on the following day left for Brindisi in Italy with two thousand five hundred Polish troops. I was on normal duty again, but when compared to the strains of being in enemy territory, on guard and afraid for my life every minute, it seemed like a holiday in a hotel. I was completely in charge of security on the ship, had my own personal cabin and spent my free time sunbathing on the top deck.

Not that I had nothing to do! As we came alongside the Italian coast in the Adriatic, one of my men came and reported that there had been an incident on the middle decks of the ship in the main latrine. This latrine was basically a long bar on which the men sat. Below there was a trough filled with running water. It turned out that some of the men had built a paper boat and loaded it with more paper, had set it alight and had floated it along the trough. The backsides of the unsuspecting men sitting on the latrine had been burned. I could hardly keep a straight face - and let the men responsible go with a warning. War is really a mixture of farce and tragedy - here I was warning these idiots about burning their comrades' backsides, and a few weeks before I had seen a woman I loved (and whom I myself should have killed) poisoned before my eyes and had shot her murderer.

I returned with the boat and my men to Port Said to pick up another load of troops. For the time, my life was uneventful; but not, of course, for long.

Chapter 19

THE THIRD MISSION

I was still shuttling to and fro between Port Said and Italy, happy with my little kingdom; I sunbathed, sorted out minor disputes, and quite enjoyed myself. Then, on arrival at Bari from Port Said in the second week of June 1944, orders were waiting for me. I had to report again to Intelligence HQ. This was now in Mottola, near Taranto in southern Italy.

Once again my Commanding Officer greeted me with that big smile, and once again I was told that everything was going to be simple, really only a game. Well, I did not believe that, I knew what had happened last time; but I did not say so. He told me that I would take off from outside Bari, and would be dropped just outside the Swiss Border in the southern part of Germany, after which the plane would return to Bari. I would have my colleague Josph with me again; he had just returned to the allied lines, guided by the partisans, after successfully accomplishing his own mission. My Commanding Officer said that Josph had learnt a lot from me, and had actually requested to join me if I went on a mission which required two agents. "He obviously thinks a lot of you," my commander concluded, "and therefore, since he has asked, and since I have received this request, I have decided that you can go together." It was all settled, and he poured out two glasses of vodka and proposed a toast to the success of the mission and to a safe return.

We had hardly finished when in came Josph Sikora, whom I had last seen when we had parachuted from the Super Fortress over Hamburg. He was very happy to see me, and shook my hand so firmly I had to tell him to ease up. Three more glasses of vodka had been poured, and were now handed round. Yet again we drank to a successful mission and safe return; after which he invited us to be seated, and started to explain what was to happen. We would go by Dakota over the Adriatic Sea, then over northern Italy near Venice, and then to the area where our mission was to take place. He turned to me and said that, since I was a veteran, he was sure he need not add too much about how I was to manage it. I in turn said I would tell him about my whole plan in advance as far as I could.

We then interrupted our talk and went over to the officers' mess for a meal; it was pointed out that it might be a few days before we had a good meal again. We gossiped over lunch about this and that, and then we returned to the commandant's office for a detailed briefing. He produced maps, one on the general layout of the journey and a second which was an ordnance map of the area where the mission was to be carried out. He brought out an envelope of pictures. These pictures were of a chalet, located about sixty miles north of the Swiss border, near a town called St. Anton. In the early days of the war, the people living in this chalet had supplied us with very important intelligence reports. However, the last signal was over two months earlier, and nothing positive had been received since then, though attempts had been made to contact them via other intelligence sources in the area.

However, the intelligence people were fairly sure that they still possessed valuable information, and we were being sent in to get it, and we could take what action we liked as long as that information came back. Our commandant also stressed that there must be some very good reason for not receiving any more information from these people, and that we should therefore look out for trouble. It could be that they had been discovered and executed. He then showed us photographs of the interior of the chalet and its surrounds. He told us that in the basement of the house there was a secret hideout in which there was a shortwave radio and classified information which had to be sent to our command. If there were any difficulties, we were to forget about the people and just try to retrieve those documents and bring them back.

The commandant then gave us a short pep talk; blowing up my ego by saying that he imagined I needed no instructions about the return journey, which I must now know by heart. He then told Josph to watch me and learn from my attitudes and behaviour. (That made me laugh inside, since the commandant had no idea how often I was terrified to death on these missions, and how often my nerves came near to breaking point.) The fact was he was trying to nerve both of us up, myself by saying how high his opinion of me was, and Josph by emphasising that he would be under the guidance of someone he respected and who could be trusted.

After this, we were sent off to our quarters to discuss what we had been told, to study all the information again, and generally impress it

on our minds. A meal would be provided in our quarters; later in the
day we would hear of the time of departure and get clothing to wear on
our mission. We found that we would both travel in German uniform,
myself as a Ober-feldwebel (Staff Sergeant) and Josph as a Korperlich
(Corporal). My name was to be Hanz Kopytnik and Josph's was to be
Robert Hadych. Their identities and background were taken from
German prisoners of war captured by the Polish forces. From the
moment we received our new identities, I suggested that we converse
in German only, to give us the feeling of our new selves. The people
who we were to contact (if they were still alive) were a middle aged
couple, called Gustav and Helga Schienberg. Gustav was serving as a
border guard on the frontier between Germany and Switzerland,
whilst Helga was a local midwife. They had no children and the nearest
chalet to theirs was about one and a half miles away. Actually, in spite
of the commandant's warning, I really began to feel there would be no
trouble.

We completed our study of the background to the mission,
continuously conversing in German, memorising all the photographs
and documents. Josph never spoke to me in Polish, unlike on the first
mission; he was learning. At 1600 hours the commandant came in and
said: "If you haven't memorised everything by now, it is too late. You
must change into your uniforms and have a last meal, then, in one
hour, the transport will be waiting to take you to Bari." He then
ordered the butler to bring the uniforms and the food; but before he
did that he asked us whether we had any particular wishes as to what
we should have. Actually, when you considered there was a war on, we
always ate well, so we said we would have whatever was ready. After
the meal, we made final preparations for our departure; and we drove
directly to the airfield on the outskirts of Bari, and climbed into our
Dakota. The aircraft's engines were already running and we had no
sooner boarded than it started moving out for takeoff.

At the beginning of the journey, we were both very quiet, but after
about half-an-hour we went through our mission again, still talking in
German. By the time we reached Venice, the night had completely
closed in and it was very dark. About one hour later, the navigator told
us we were only one minute away from the 'drop zone', so we put on
our parachutes and hitched up our safety lines. The doors were opened
and the red light appeared, which meant we should jump in fifteen
seconds. We stood in the doorway of the Dakota with our eyes on the
light. The pilot reduced speed, and as soon as the light changed to

green, I jumped, with Josph following me.

We landed on the slope of a hill between high trees. I managed to hit the ground with no problem, but Josph's parachute got tangled in the trees and he ended up suspended about two metres up. He tried to pull the parachute free, but in the end had to punch his safety release button and jumped down. We checked our Schmeissers and grenades, and then proceeded towards the chalet, and within 45 to 50 minutes we were there, hidden in trees about fifty yards from the walls.

We sat there and took a good look; and I began to feel very worried. Somehow, everything was just too quiet, and I had a strong premonition that something was very wrong. After discussion, it was decided that I go to the lower side of the house (it was built on a slope) where there was access to the basement and the secret compartment where the papers were kept; if they were there, I would take them. Josph would watch the front door meantime for any sign of trouble. I went down and got into the basement without difficulty, and quickly located the secret compartment. The radio transmitter was no longer there. There were a few rolls of fire logs stored in the basement, and I decided to move them. After moving two rolls of logs, I found a fairly large package of papers hidden behind them. Without delay, I went back to Josph, who was waiting in our temporary hideout in the trees. I told him what I had found, and we decided to wait for a while to see what happened.

A short while later, our caution was rewarded. A German soldier, a fairly short little chap, came out of the chalet, sub-machine gun at the ready. He checked out all the surrounds of the house very carefully and then went back into the house. He spoke to someone inside, and we heard him say that there was nobody about. With that, the house suddenly erupted with laughter and loud conversation. It was obvious that something had happened, that the couple were either dead or no longer there. It was also likely that the Germans were expecting someone to show up, since the chalet was in peaceful country far from any fighting; yet intensive precautions were being taken.

We could have just left; we had basically got we had come for, but we were young and full of fight; we decided that as the house was full of Germans who were only too willing to kill us, we would return the compliment and exterminate the lot of them. The plan was to creep up to the house and each throw two grenades simultaneously - four of them ought to settle the matter. We approached the house in dead silence, with our grenades ready, moving slowly, very tense. We

crawled underneath the windows of the chalet. Josph prepared his
grenades by taking both pins out, and I did the same.

On a signal from me, we both threw our grenades in through the
window and ran off as fast as we could in an easterly direction. We cut
it rather fine, for before we had gone twenty five yards the blast came,
and we were literally blown into the air however, we landed a few
yards further on without any damage apart from a few bruises. (Yes, I
was really tough in those days.) Looking back, we could hardly believe
our eyes, for the house had been completely destroyed and debris was
flying all over the place, in a mushroom of smoke and dust and noise. I
could not understand how four grenades could destroy the whole
building, even a wooden one, and it is still a mystery to me. Maybe
there were explosives inside which our grenades set off; not that we
worried about it at that moment, just looked at each other in great
surprise and legged it energetically, trying to put as much distance as
possible between us and the ruins.

All the Germans had been killed, and nobody followed us. We
walked as fast as we could, and must have covered between twelve to
fifteen miles before we stopped to rest. We stood watch in turn, so that
each of us could have some sleep, and in the late afternoon, after we
had eaten our iron rations, we discussed what to do next, and decided
to cross into Switzerland and travel through the eastern part of that
country towards Italy. This we did, travelling always in open country
and avoiding all settlements and towns on the route, for we were still in
German uniform, and would have been arrested by the Swiss police.
When we came to the Italian border, we waited till darkness before
crossing, which we did without difficulty. Then we dumped our
German jackets in some bushes and marched towards the nearest
village; which we entered with confidence, since both of us spoke
fluent Italian.

Again without difficulty, we found people who volunteered to
contact the local partisans for us, and these men guided us through the
mountains and handed us over to another partisan group near a town
called Barcis. From there we were shepherded to the large town of
Treviso, where the partisan HQ was situated, and where I could
communicate with my friends at the HQ at Mottola.

The partisans readily agreed to allow us to communicate with our
HQ. However, the radio was not kept in the town, but in a hideout
outside, in open country - because of the danger from German
detector stations. We left the town with the local group leader and a

small band of about fifteen men. We were approaching the hideout where the radio was concealed; but suddenly the group leader stopped us and ordered silence. We could hear someone talking inside the hideout. After a few moments, two men, including a group leader, (not the local man), went forward to creep round the hideout and listen. After a while there was loud shouting and two shots. We were all galvanised into action and ran forward. As we crowded the door of the hideout, which was just a makeshift shack in the woods, we found the group leader who had carried out the scouting expedition. He had a gun in his hand and the wireless operator was dead.

"He was transmitting to the Germans," said the man with the gun. "I don't need to tell you how we treat traitors." We relaxed - the incident was over; it shows what kind of world I was living in then when I tell you that it was just an incident, and I hardly thought of it again until I came to write this book - so many worse things happened to me.

After that, another man took over the radio, and contacted our HQ. We were told that in two days time, there would be a boat patrolling at about 25 knots south east of Ravenna. If we failed to meet it, it would return every twenty four hours for the next five days; and the partisan command had received orders to secure our safe passage.

We were issued with Italian identities, and travelled as Italian citizens along the main road straight into Ravenna, and stayed in a safe place with a family which supported the partisans. In the late afternoon we went to a small fishing village on the south side of Ravenna, where about a dozen small boats were preparing to go out for the night's fishing. There were no German guards, so we just mixed with the fishermen, and went out on one of the boats; which were mostly old-fashioned sailing craft, only one having an engine. We stood out from the coast towards the area where we were to be picked up. We got there at 1830 hours, but the boat did not come, and we thought that perhaps something had happened to it. However, after 2200 hours we went with the one boat that had an engine, and they motored further south, and shortly afterwards we heard a powerful engine in the distance.

The boat soon came in sight, and slowed down; the crew all had sub-machine guns which were aimed at us - they were taking no chances. It turned out to be a largish naval motor boat with a Polish crew. We transferred to it, and the captain of the fishing boat was handed an envelope with a substantial reward for himself and his crew and another envelope to be delivered to the partisan HQ. Seconds later, with the engine at full throttle, we started on our journey back, and by midday on the following day had reached a seaside town called Barletta; and there on the quayside was our Commanding Officer, awaiting our arrival!

He welcomed us, and took us directly to the Polish NAAFI, where we had a very substantial dinner and a few very essential glasses of vodka, and I can tell you, we really appreciated it all. After a mission the tension relaxes and there is a wonderful feeling of security and leisure. After this, he told us that after we had filed a full report, we both had seven days' leave. In the event, both Josph and I decided to go to Capri together, since we got on very well, and had a wonderful holiday there in beautiful surroundings. After our adventurous little jaunt, we had certainly earned our rest.

Chapter 20

THE FOURTH MISSION

While I was on police duty outside Pescara, I received orders to report to Intelligence Headquarters. The front on the western side of Italy was then north of Rome and the Allied forces were pushing hard towards Florence. The city of Pescara was already in the hands of Polish forces and the front was near St. Benedetto. However, all the hard work I was carrying out was not my immediate concern. What mattered to me was a summons to do another mission. I was not to be in German uniform this time, and would wear British uniform - but it did mean going behind the lines, and the whole operation was basically undercover. The matter was explained to me as follows:

We had an agent in Germany - the only name I ever had for him was Rudolf. The SS were extremely active, now that the war was going so badly for Germany, and many of Rudolf's accomplices and contacts had already been caught and shot. It was only a matter of time before he was caught himself. Seeing what was happening, he had already left Germany, heading for the Allied lines. However, he had only been able to get as far as San Remo, in North Italy. He could very easily have contacted the partisans, who could have got him to safety with no trouble - but he was not known to them, and obviously they were very careful with whom they dealt.

And that was where I came in. I was to travel to North Italy with an English officer as helper, contact Rudolf, and bring him to safety. I was to rendezvous with him at the home of a couple who were sympathetic to the Allied cause. At the same time, I was to collect a package of valuable information which the couple had for us, thus doing two jobs at once.

I agreed to go. But there was a need for speed. My English colleague, whom I had met while receiving my briefing, pointed out that we would have to be dropped at San Remo, on the West Coast, by a submarine. Unfortunately, if we had waited for a submarine, we would have been too late, and the Englishman pushed them into letting us go by torpedo boat. So that was how I went to sea again! We went up by the West coast in the torpedo boat, travelling North, and actually saw the lights of the beaches where the Romans traditionally go to bathe, and where Mark Antony, according to legend, said goodbye to Cleopatra after Caesar had been murdered in the Senate, and she had had to escape to Egypt with her son, Caesarion.

About nine o'clock in the evening we noticed a light ahead of us, flashing signals in Morse. The crew went to action stations at once, manning the machine guns in case it was a trick, and Germans were waiting for us. We reduced speed to a crawl over the smooth water, and soon we were alongside the submarine that would take us on the next leg of our journey. The submarine took us on our way, travelling underwater. After two-and-a-half hours it came to the point where we were to be dropped off. They half surfaced, so as to show themselves as little as possible. We were launched into the water in a rubber dinghy with final instructions as to which lights to aim for so that we would arrive at San Remo.

As we pulled away to the shore we could see the sub floating on the water, illuminated by the bright moonlight - a lonely feeling. They would soon be back home, while we were off on our own, far from any help, dependent entirely on our wits and courage. We paddled in the direction laid down for us, and about half an hour later we were about two hundred yards from the shore, and could see the German shore patrols walking up and down the waterfront. We holed and sank the dinghy under us in shallow water. In a few minutes we could feel the sea bed under our feet and cautiously waded ashore, towing waterproof bags with our uniforms in them.

We found a quiet corner and changed out of our wet clothes, which we threw away. Then we set off to find the house, whose location we had memorised from maps and aerial photographs. I was now dressed in a British uniform, and carried a tommygun and a few grenades.

We had no difficulty locating the house where the couple lived fairly easily. It was a few miles north of San Remo, on the southern side of a large hill. There were few houses near it, it was basically outside town. The house itself was wooden, rather like a typical Swiss chalet. We had been told that Rudolf would be waiting outside. It may be that the couple had not even been told about Rudolf - he would just turn up. Frankly, they did not need to know, and what they did not need to know, they would not be told. That was and is how Intelligence works.

However, when we arrived, there was a distinct problem. We knocked on the door, and instead of being greeted by the couple we had come to see, we ran right into a noisy party - and the guests were high-ranking German officers and Italian Fascists. For a moment we gaped at each other, both sides completely taken by surprise.

They knew we were enemies, for we wore British uniform. Well, this was one of those times when quick reactions were called for, and I threw two grenades into the house, and my partner did the same. The house shook with the explosions, there were shouts and screams.

And we - we had to run for our lives. However, we kept our heads to some extent. They would naturally expect us to run south, back towards the Allied lines. But we went north - and thus evaded them. We went straight up the steep side of the hill behind the house, and when we had gone some distance, and felt a little safer, we paused in order to think and re-assess the whole situation. Looking back, we could still see the house, which was ablaze. The Germans were wasting ammunition - there was plenty of light automatic fire. Obviously some of them had survived the grenades.

Before we could really make any plans, we heard someone call: "Rudolf, Rudolf!" It was the agent we had come to meet - that was his recognition sign. We replied with our codeword, "Departed, departed!" There were a few tense moments as we waited, listening for any unwelcome sounds - like soldiers lying in hiding. In this situation you could never be sure that Rudolf had not been captured, tortured - and made to talk. In which case we could be meeting with the Gestapo instead of Rudolf! However, soon we were sure there was no danger, and then Rudolf's voice called softly right in front of us.

Once he was identified he had to give us a small parcel wrapped in waterproof cloth. He asked what plans we had, for we were essentially in charge of him from then on. So suspicious and paranoid is the intelligence world that it was only at that point that I learned that my British colleague was not coming back with us, as he had to accomplish another mission further north. Rudolf and I said goodbye to him and I asked Rudolf to follow me on the return journey. Later that day I got some civilian clothes from some friendly Italians and once again moved into the role of a partisan.

What happened to the couple we were supposed to meet? God knows. They may have been killed by our grenades - we never knew. This kind of encounter is so frequent in war - you just never know the end result of your own actions. It turned out that Rudolf had arrived at the house, saw the party going on, and had kept clear and kept an eye out for us.

After that, we made our way south, walking through the mountains, using map and compass. The next thing that happened was that the Germans gave us a helping hand! We walked into a village, looking for food. While we were there, the Gestapo arrived and began confisacating all the transport. I and Rudolf were on a farm, where there was only a woman in charge. When the Gestapo came round, I told Rudolf that he must pretend to be my deaf and dumb brother. I said that I was the woman's husband. My Italian was very good by this time, and I had no trouble with them at all.

The Gestapo agent was only interested in finding whether I could drive. I told him that I could, and so could Rudolf, in spite of his "disability." The Germans were very short of drivers, and under great pressure. So immediately Rudolf and I were conscripted as drivers - and told to drive exactly in the direction which we were heading - towards my mountains, towards Florence. We drove well, and obeyed orders exactly, and had no difficulties. As soon as we were within ten miles of Florence, we decided to make a run for the partisans on Monte Giove.

The following morning, the Germans were attacking the partisans to clear the way for their retreat. We sneaked off - in all the confusion, with soldiers here and there and nobody knowing really what was happening, it was easy for us just to slip away. No guard was put on us. We got up in the hills, and I went straight to partisan headquarters, where we were well received, for everyone remembered me. The partisans were packing up their headquarters to move. The German attack was making things very hot for them, and it was best for them to move into Florence, which had been declared an open city, and would therefore not be shelled or bombed by either side. Very soon the Allies would be there anyway.

So Rudolf and I split up the packet of papers we carried, just as a precaution, and marched with the partisans, six hundred of us all told. The partisans knew the country well, and I did not anticipate any trouble. We had to descend from the mountain, and then we would be on the outskirts of Florence.

Well, it did not happen like that. As we were on the flank of the mountain, very near to the spot where I had hidden those two bars of gold, only a few months before (though it seemed much longer, for so many things had happened in the meantime), we were ambushed. War is often so boring - until it suddenly becomes terrifying, often within seconds. We were just marching along, one leg moving after another in the usual way, through lovely mountain country, when the guns opened up. That was where it happened, four miles from Florence.

The firing came from German bunkers, very near, and disguised as rocks, so we had not noticed them. I and my immediate comrades were safe only because they were, in fact, so very near. The flame from the barrels of the 88 mm guns, and there must have been six or seven of them, went a few feet over our heads. They could not depress the barrels low enough to hit us - that was all that saved us.

I ran a little bit down the valley, trying to get away from the guns. And then uphill, past many rocks - many of which were actually bunkers, which, as I have said, were disguised to look like rocks. It was very steep, and I had to half run, half climb. All the time, the guns were hammering away. We were desperate for somewhere to hide. I and a few more behind me, I saw a big rock, which was actually partly a bunker. We could not be seen, we were too low, but the guns were firing over our heads. There was a little bush....

I jumped behind the bush - and fell down, down into a big hole - and before I knew what had happened, bang, bang, bang, bang, four men jumped in behind me, desperate for a hiding place and following my lead. We lay there, panting and saying nothing. Outside, the firing went on and on, scattering the partisan column, many of whom were killed. I never saw Rudolf again and of course the papers he had carried were lost. I expect that he was killed there and then on the mountainside.

So there we were, stuck right under a German bunker, with Germans all round us in their fortifications. The hole under the rock was just big enough for the five of us to lie in and move about a little. I looked around carefully, and had a shock - it was, in fact, the very place where I had buried the gold. I was lying there, in terror of my life, hungry and thirsty, on top of a fortune! Well, that was that - what irony! It was nearly daybreak - and we could not get out. We lay there, hoping to be able to get out in the evening - but when evening came, there were too many Germans, and we stayed there. The next day was the same, and the next.

The time after that was, perhaps, my worst time in the whole war - even the Russian labour camp would have been preferable. There was nothing to do - yet we were constantly tense. There were Germans all round us - we could hear them moving about, talking. At any moment, one might have idly looked down the hole and found us. We just lay there, two Russians, one Frenchman, and one Italian, and one Pole, myself, I was the only one who had any food. I had some iron rations and some dried fruit which I kept under my belt. I told my comrades that they could have one piece of fruit a day, plus a little water. That was all. We had to save it.

And so we lay and lay, while Germans walked to and fro across the little valley. The front was very close to us, and the guns of both sides fired constantly, the shells passing over our heads. And it was here, peeping out of our hole through the bushes, that I saw a remarkable thing - there was a double loud explosion - but in the air, not on the ground. Two shells must have actually met and exploded in mid-air - a one in many thousands chance. Many of my friends have never believed this story - but I know what I saw and heard.

We spent 21 days in that hole. We thought constantly about food. Within our sight there was a farmhouse. No doubt there was plenty of food there - but we also knew, having kept observation on the place, that there were plenty of Germans there as well. However, we observed that on our side of the farmhouse there was a garden with fruit trees. And one night during our second week in the hole, I and one of the others crept out to forage.

I crept out on my hands and knees from under the rock and began to slide down the steep slope towards the garden. It was a moonless night; however, the sky was clear, and the outline of the farmhouse was clearly visible. My companion was to wait at the entrance to the hole until I reached the boundary wall of the house and gave him the signal that all was clear. If I did not signal, then he knew there was trouble, and was to stay where he was. Checking that the coast was clear, I signalled, and then made for the fruit trees, listening for the slightest sound. I did spot one German guard sitting on a bench, and went back to the boundary wall to wait for my friend and warn him.

After that we went forward, wriggling round the guard very quietly. Reaching the fruit trees, we pulled down thirty or forty pears. Then we heard a dog barking in the farmyard, and we retreated as quickly as possible. On our return, I took over the pears my friend had been carrying and kept them in a central store. I gave each man two pears per day, and told them this was their ration. In fact, I think the choice of the pears was not very fortunate for one of the men. He died a few days later, and I think the pears may have caused it; they are not the best food to have when one is half starved. However, they gave us some relief and after the death had decreased our numbers I doubled the ration - two pears in the morning and two in the evening. At least they contained some moisture, which was very welcome, for we suffered terribly from thirst as well.

I kept a diary, which unfortunately was burnt in a fire in the 1960's. The pages of the diary showed how I had deteriorated - I was a mental case from starvation, and every sentence exchanged between us was about bread, about food, about water. Eventually I decided that I had had enough. I would rather risk death by bullets rather than starve any longer. Two days before one of the Russians had died, and we had to shift him right underneath the rock as far away from us as possible. We had earlier excavated a little more room for ourselves - partly in order to be more comfortable, partly to pass the time. But in spite of all we could do, the body stank, and added to our misery.

I told the Italian I was going that night, and that evening another Russian died. The Frenchman was too ill to move, so it was only the Italian, and me who were fit enough to make the attempt. We would have to leave the ill man behind, and hope the front moved forward quickly enough for him to be rescued. So round about midnight I put all my papers under my beret, and just took four grenades and a Luger with me, crawled out of the hole, and set off down the hill, with the Italian following.

It was a very steep hill. You could not see what was at the bottom, for there were small trees there, but it did not look too deep. That day, we had actually been able to look out from our hole, two kilometres away, across the River Arno, to the American lines. And at night you could see the flash of their machine guns - and the flashes of the German guns as they fired over our heads.

One thing I had not reckoned with was my own weakness, after twenty-one days with little food and no exercise. I took two or three steps, and my legs gave way. I cannot even remember how I went - mostly on hands and knees, I think. I crawled down towards the river, slowly, slowly. I was actually half upright when the solid ground came to an end, and I fell over the edge and was falling - I seemed to fall for ages.

I dropped on top of some trees, and the branches held me up for a while then slowly gave way. I did not dare move. Then the trees took the decision for me, and I dropped again, splash, into an icy cold stream. Lovely. Salvation. I drank and drank and drank that lovely water - never look down on water as a drink, it is fantastic.

I was still drinking when splash, in front of me, came a man - it was the Italian fellow. After a few quiet words with him, I began to walk downstream. The water was about twelve inches deep, so I could walk, without any difficulty. After I had walked about half a kilometre, I passed a small cliff, in which there was a hole. There were some people there, and they were talking German. Actually, incredibly enough, I met one of them later - he was Polish - fighting with the free Polish forces. His name was Edward Hunka, and he actually came from Zimna Woda, my home village! But of course at the time I thought he and the others were German soldiers.

I walked on a bit further, and the bushes that lined the river vanished. Day was breaking, and in front of me there was this beautiful garden of tomatoes. My first aim was to get among these lovely big tomatoes and stuff myself. I don't know how many I ate, but I must have eaten quite a few. And then I fell asleep, exhausted.

When I woke, I could hear German voices, I could hear their steps. Peering through the tomato plants. I could see a German platoon, sub-machine guns in their hands, passing by. One of them came to pick tomatoes, and the commander shouted at him, and from what he said, I knew there were some booby traps in the tomatoes. After that I said to myself: "I must be careful."

Nearby there was a bridge on the road from Florence to Pontasieve - I had known it in my partisan days. It had already been mined, and the stream was very shallow and dry - well, nearly dry. It was only a few hundred yards away, and it took me nearly 24 hours to get there. There were bodies - Italians and Germans lying all over and I was lying between those bodies. Sometimes I crawled, very very slowly. Once or twice Germans studied me. Try to imagine what it was like, lying facing the sky and pretending to be dead. One came right up to me, and actually trod on me. I could have screamed with the pain, but of course I had to lie absolutely still and not make a sound. In the end, he moved away.

Most of the time, I just lay there and surveyed everything I could. My object was to get across the bridge. On the right was a millhouse, and on the left a little garden. I could see on the left a square rainwater outlet, a drain two or three feet from the ground. Finally I managed to reach it, for it offered some shelter. I knew I could not turn round in it, so I went in legs first. I pulled in stones after me, and built a wall to hide me from anyone who looked in from the outside. I could hear rats scuttling about in the drain, but I ignored them.

Actually, I felt a lot better. I had had plenty of tomatoes, and water, and I was no longer in that stinking hole. And I went to sleep till late afternoon, when I woke up, pushed away the stones, and went to the entrance. I could see no one about on the German side. There was gunfire in the distance, but mostly it was quiet.

As my eyes were resting casually on the kerb of the pavement, the kerb exploded in a rush of golden flame two feet high, and there was the crash of an explosion. It was the Americans who were shelling me - they had spotted me and were trying to knock me out. I thought: "That is amazing, I have survived all the Germans and Russians could do, only to be killed by the Americans, my allies!"

I scuttled off back into my hole, and waited for night. Around midnight, there was a beautiful starry sky, with no moon. I crawled from my hole, and lay in the water with only my feet showing. The water was calm here, in a big pool just above some cataracts - though I did not know that. There were a lot of bodies floating in the water. I was just thinking, planning my journey across, when that stupid Italian fellow with whom I had shared the hole, he shows up. I do not know what the hell he had been doing with himself. But he sees me waiting by the river, and does not realise whom I am. He shouted: "Halto che vola - halt who goes there" and fired his gun, bang bang bang, right over my head.

I froze stiff, stayed completely still. He jumped into the river, and guns opened up from both sides, German and American. He was literally cut to bits, blasted apart, his body disintegrating over the surface of the water. I really nearly lost hope. For the moment, everyone on both sides of the river was my enemy. Everyone just shot at anything that moved. I felt there just was no chance of my getting to safety. But old habits die hard, and I kept trying. Over to my left there was a fence, obviously built to hold back the erosion of the bank, where long grass hung down over the bank itself. There was space for me to hide there, and I moved over there very slowly. I took three hours to move three yards, because I was playing dead again, and moved only fractions of an inch at a time.

At last I reached it, I put my head above the water under the long grass so that I could breathe. And there I stayed, standing in the water, for twenty four hours, all through the next day, until darkness came again. My only company were the water rats, who came sniffing around my face, quite unafraid, for I was so still. I could not even brush them away, for I did not want to make ripples in the water. There were so many eyes looking at the river, and they were all hostile as far as I was concerned.

That evening, I began to think how I was going to move about in the water unnoticed. I have said that there were many bodies lying in the water. I kept a careful eye on them and noted how fast they were moving in the current, for I had an idea how I might use them. I noticed towards evening a body coming very slowly towards me, a body of a German soldier When it came level with me it was not quite dark, so I could not move, but I got hold of it and kept it.

When darkness had really come, about midnight, I got between the legs of the corpse, so that my head was hidden in his crutch. I started pushing the body downstream gently, out into the centre where the water was moving a bit faster. That took me half-an-hour, perhaps a bit more, to do twenty yards. Then the body was moving faster, and I was pushing a bit faster still, then I was standing in the river, moving with it. This took a long time, nearly all night in fact, for I had to move so very slowly, so that to the casual observer it just looked as if another body was moving with the river.

Eventually, as I stood there, I looked towards the German side, and saw about two dozen machine guns emplaced there in concrete bunkers, heavy ones, 20mm jobs. I could not see the American guns, they were hidden behind barbed wire and hedges. Through the lessening darkness, I began to make out a chapel on the American side, yellowish in colour with a red roof and a big tree. From behind me, like in a picture, the sun was rising with this golden starlight - like a stream of light coming - and I prayed.

And all of a sudden, my legs begin to lose their balance. I did not know why, but my legs were going faster and faster, and I could not catch up with them. I was walking on the river bed. In fact, there were cataracts ahead, and the current at the bottom was getting stronger as it rushed towards them. I kept tight hold of the body, which was still my only protection Then I hit my legs very badly. They were badly scratched and skinned, and the water took charge. I was swept away.

The next thing I knew, I was lying between hundreds of bodies on the American side of the river. The sun was shining. I could see as clearly as anything - I could see people clearly on the German side, I could see them moving in the bunkers through the gun slits. I had to move. I was still in sight of the German guns.

Nearby was a big tree. Three coils of barbed wire stretched in front of it, the beginnings of the American defences. I had to get over them. In my weakened, giddy state I felt I just had not got a chance. On the other hand, if I stayed where I was, sooner or later death would find me. I tightened my muscles so much that they were really painful, and picked myself up. And then.....I leapt..... and fractions of seconds later I was over the wire. I really do not know how I did it, even now, but my body knew it was really necessary - and managed it. In an emergency. one can do wonderful things.

I fell on the other side. and then hell opened up, an incredible inferno of noise as the guns opened up. And then my body just gave up - I blanked out. The next thing I remember is lying in hospital in Florence. with my Commanding Officer sitting by me. I was a skeleton. For.three weeks I lived on noodles and soft foods until my full health came back. And that was the end of it, that last bastard mission which nearly killed me a dozen times over. But stubborn men are hard to kill - and I was alive.

Chapter 21

BACK TO THE RANKS

After my last mission, I had had enough. But soon after my recovery, I was asked to do another one, and this request indirectly ended my career in Intelligence. As a matter of fact, the way it all ended made me very angry. The fact was that when I was asked to go on this next mission, I asked them why I was being chosen for these missions at all. They replied that of course one reason was that I spoke fluent German, but also went on to say that I was chosen because killing was no problem to me, since I had no emotions. I was furious - I felt a great deal more than they gave me credit for, and after my last series of adventures and ordeals, my nerves were completely shattered.

I refused to go on any more missions, point blank. They could not make me go on another, since these missions were strictly for volunteers - but they gave me some disagreeable duties to show me how they felt. They sent me off to "convalesce" - which meant police duty on a convoy to Brindisi. Later, I was sent to Rome to work as a military policeman there. What a shambles that was; Rome was full of soldiers of all nationalities, all sorts and conditions of men, and they were far from home, often depressed, and frequently drunk. The result was endless trouble.

I was supposed to be on CID duty, but really I was part of what amounted to a squad of riot police. We used to stay in our quarters at the Albergo (Hotel) Nationale, drinking tea and coffee and chatting, till the alarm bell rang. And then we were off - generally speaking, I had to go when there were Polish troops involved in trouble. But of course, when there was a general alarm, we all had to go. As a rule, the Poles gave us, their own military police, no trouble, and would come to order as soon as we arrived - on one or two occasions they even sought our protection. The only exceptions were the commandos, all big men, over six feet tall every one, who cared for nothing and nobody, and would fight with knives, not their fists. We had some big fights with them.

One occasion I shall never forget is when we were called out on a general alarm. It turned out that two regiments of soldiers out for a good time had arrived in Rome, and were streaming past the Coliseum from the Piazza Venezia, in opposite directions. Each lot was looking out for a good time, and each had their own ideas as to where the good time was. Someone pushed someone, someone insulted someone else, and a terrific fight started, maybe four hundred or six hundred men all fighting, with two streets blocked.

The American military police were out in strength. They arrived in three GMC's (open police vehicles, like trucks with no tops, which mounted light machine guns in a turret) and behind them were three more GMC's full of military police of other nationalities. I was in the one before last. We all carried tommy guns, pistols and so on, as a matter of course. What a scene - I have never seen anything quite like it. A great mass of seething, sweating, punching men. It was impossible to quiet them by ordinary means, and so we fired over their heads with our tommy guns to try and quieten them.

They took no notice, and the riot continued. In the end the Americans lost patience and opened fire with the mounted light machine guns on their GMC's, and killed quite a lot of their own men. What futility - they were not even killed fighting the enemy. Of course that broke it up, and the crowd dispersed, leaving about twenty or twenty-five bodies behind.

Rome was completely incredible in those days. The Italian economy was in ruins, the population was starving, many families lacked a breadwinner, and there were women and even children in the streets who would make love in exchange for a can of corned beef or any kind of food. It really put me off sex to see these hungry desperate people so ready to degrade themselves.

Mind you, there were moments of humour, even in the military police. I can remember one time when we were on duty up in the North, at Porto San Georgio. We had a call from the stationmaster south of the town, between there and Pedasso, and they said a troop train had stopped there, why, they did not know, and there was trouble with the men on it. We were just south of Porto San Georgio ourselves. We all, literally everybody, dashed out. When we got to the train, the nature of the trouble was very simple and straightforward. The train was full of Scottish soldiers, all dead drunk, and very disorderly, lying around everywhere - the train was in an indescribable mess, vomit and spilled drink everywhere. The carriages smelt to high heaven.

Our CO said: "We can't arrest them all. Just take the officers." So we carried them back and put them in cells. They were so drunk they had no idea what had happened. Then we asked the stationmaster to lock all the wagons. Half of us went to sleep, while the other half, sub-machine guns at the ready, guarded the train full of Scotsmen. Luckily, they were too drunk to make much real trouble.

The next day, there was a terrible banging from those officers in the cells. (We had locked them up in the local Italian police station.) They called from one to another: "Jack where are you?" "Hello, hello." "What's happening?" And so on and so on. We went into the cells, and poured ice cold water over the officers, a bucket each, to finish sobering them up. "What right have you to treat us like this?" said the captain.

Our lieutenant replied: "Sir, the same right as you have a right to get drunk. Do you know how you walked here?"

"Certainly, straight ahead."

"No, sir. Two men carried you."

The captain sobered up, and asked what damage had been done. We told him we would show him, but first, he had to straighten himself up, for he was going to face his men. By that time, Captain Wisniewski, a senior officer in the military police, had arrived from Ancona, 40 kilometres away. When the captain saw the state of the train, he became more apologetic, saying that they had been in the battle line for three months. "It is our first week off, two whole regiments. We were supposed to look after them, but you would not be a Scotsman if you did not drink." That was what he said. Well, we all knew what battle was like, and Captain Wisniewski decided to be lenient. It was agreed that if the officer saw the train was cleaned up and on it's way in two hours, the matter would be forgotten.

The Scots officers lined the men all up by the train, all at attention. The captain asked one six-foot soldier with ginger hair, whose mouth was crumpled up - he obviously had no teeth: "Where are your teeth?"

The soldier said: "I don't know sir."

"Where did you miss them?"

"I didn't miss them."

"Where are they?"

"In Rome."

The captain agreed that Rome, two hundred kilometres away, was too long a journey just to collect missing teeth. Well, after the inspection, the station master gave them two dozen buckets. The sea

was only 20 yards away, and they brought salty water, washed the
train. The engine was at the station, and it pulled them out of the layby,
and they left. We were only too glad to see the last of them.

One of my more peculiar duties in Porto San Giorgio was to check
medical cards in the local brothels. All the girls had to have them, and
the brothel could not open until those cards had been stamped by us to
certify them all VD free. Three of us used to go. There were five to
fifteen prostitutes, some of them beautiful. One or two used to put
their arms round my neck, and say: "Come to me after the war, be my
protector, I will give you anything you want." However, I was not very
tempted to take them up on their offer.

The duties I had in the police were varied. Sometimes it was traffic
control duty near the front line, sometimes detective work, trying to
control corruption, which war seems to give birth to just as gardens
grow flowers. We never made more than a dent in it. The black market
in Italy was something extraordinary. Whole lorryloads of sugar or
milk or other food would be stolen and disappear. The worst army for
corruption was the American army. They had some real gangsters who
had joined, come over and deserted, operating the racket. Perhaps
they had connections with the Mafia back at home and in Italy itself.

Once, I had a dangerous confrontation with these men. One night, I
was going from Pesaro to Urbino. The bridge that linked the main road
had been blown up by Germans before their retreat, and the British
forces had provided a detour road and temporary bridge alongside the
ruins of the old bridge. As I descended towards the detour road in my
jeep, suddenly an American GI with a tommygun in his hand stepped
right in front of me, aiming at my head. As I pulled up and stopped,
two more soldiers with tommyguns came out of the bushes.

I did not even have the time to reach for my gun. He ordered me out
of the jeep; but I mustered all the calm and self control under pressure
which I had learnt through my adventures. I casually told him that if he
valued his life then he had better run off and hide. Behind me, I told
him, there was a truck with thirty Polish commandos in it. (Of course,
this was completely untrue - I was alone.) As I talked to him, the lights
from the headlamps of an oncoming vehicle appeared a short distance
down the road, and the man standing in front of my jeep signalled to
his colleagues, and all three of them disappeared into the bushes.

It took me a few seconds to compose myself - I was shaken, no
matter what I had pretended. Then I went on my way, not knowing
what the following vehicle was. After about one and a half miles I

stopped, and waited for the vehicle to be shown up by the lights near the bridge. It was an old Fiat van with the big ends knocking like hell; he could not go faster than thirty miles an hour. But grinding along like that it had sounded like a big truck, and had saved my skin.

When I got back to HQ, I told Captain Wisniewski about the incident, and he telephoned the nearest infantry regiment and they went out and searched the surrounding area all night. In the end, they captured one of the gangsters. He was interrogated for about thirty six hours, and they found he had served a prison sentence in America and had been released on parole, on condition that he served in the American forces. He had in fact deserted from his regiment and had been living rough for the last three months. His friends were also deserters of the same kind, but they had moved on and were not caught, since he had no idea where they were. They had stopped my jeep with the idea of stealing it, their own vehicle having broken down, and using it for an armed robbery they had planned.

In this incident, as at other times, I could rely on nothing but myself, the ability to stay calm, to stare into someone's eyes, willing them to believe you, to back down, to go under to your power. Maybe my ability to do this was the reason I was picked for the Special Branch. I mentioned earlier when I wrote about this that when we were interviewed, the Colonel, Polish Provost Marshall came, and he stared in our eyes, one by one, for about ninety seconds to two minutes. Then.... 'Out, out....' most of us were rejected. But not me. Maybe he saw something in me, a toughness forged by my experiences and projected through my eyes. I think so.

Chapter 22

LAST DAYS OF THE WAR

I still had a few adventures to come: For a start, I was wounded. After the battle at Ancona, about which I wrote earlier, we advanced to Senigallia, and then advanced to Pesaro, which was about twenty miles further on. That was about November - and there the front stuck, because the first snow fell then, four feet deep. The weather was bad, and past Pesaro, on the way to Cattolica and Rimini we had to cross a small river, and on the other side there were marshes, behind which was the German defence line known as Line Gotta. Every few yards, there was a heavy German bunker with a heavy gun and machine guns. Because of the marshes, tanks were useless, and it would have been suicidal to attack with infantry. So there we were, and there was I. On the 27 December, 1944, at 2pm I was directing traffic near the front line, in Pessaro, in the town square.

And as I was doing that, a shell curved in and fell in the snow without exploding, and lay there, a cylinder of golden metal, about a foot long. For all my experience, I could not move. I was frozen to the spot, looking at death lying there in the snow. In the background, tanks were passing, treads roaring through the snow and turning it to slush. Then I snapped out of it, and ran. I got only two steps when the shell exploded, and I fell.

I sat there in the snow - and a colleague ran over and asked me if I was all right. I said that I was, and he said: "Thank God." I felt rather hot, and said so; and also remarked in a matter-of-fact way that I should get back to duty. Traffic soon snarls up if left unattended! I got up - and blood began to flood out of my left boot. My puttees must have been holding it in up to then. Within a few minutes I was in an ambulance on my way back to a hospital in Senigallia. They found I had twenty-two pieces of shrapnel in my leg, some of which are still there. They held me there till 27 January 1945, and then I managed to get out, though they wanted me to stay longer. Actually, I had some trouble with the wound, for it opened again, but I managed to keep out of hospital.

At this time, at the beginning of 1945, I was given the task of teaching some Polish officers how to drive. On one occasion, a colonel was driving the truck whilst I was sitting beside him, giving him instructions. Suddenly I realised he was driving far too fast, so I gave a polite warning to slow down and apply brakes. We were just approaching a bend which curved off to the left. Instead of applying the brakes, he pressed the accelerator, and hit a steep bank on the right hand side, and the truck overturned. At this point, I would like to point out there were another eleven men, all driving trainees, on top of the lorry. When we all managed to scramble out, I said to the colonel,

"You have overturned the truck, now put it back on it's wheels." He replied that we needed a crane.

"Oh, no, you don't," I said, "We can do it ourselves." Between the thirteen of us, we raised the truck back onto it's wheels, to the great astonishment of the officers, who hardly believed their own strength. Shortly afterwards, the Chief Examiner was killed whilst taking a test with another officer, and I was given his job. In total, I taught and tested between five and ten thousand officers. Mind you, I was teaching twenty a week and testing fifty - it was not the protracted matter it is in civilian life - basically, they did most of their learning after I had given them the rudiments! Some of them were awful drivers, and caused some bad accidents afterwards. But that is war for you.

Not long after that, the front advanced to Rimini. And in Rimini I met the only man whom I had to control with a gun through all my time with the military police. He was a high ranking British officer.

I was on traffic control outside Rimini, right up on the front line. Two hundred yards down the road, German territory began, and all personnel were forbidden to proceed further unless they were actually combat troops.

And up draws a car, a frontline car with large tyres which allowed it to go across country if it had to. I stopped them, as I stopped all vehicles, and asked them where they were going. The driver replied that they were going down the road to the right, their destination being ten miles away. I told them flatly that this was not allowed.

Sitting in the car was a high ranking British officer, short, tubby, red faced, with shoulder flashes which showed a white mermaid on a red background. These meant that he was attached to the headquarters of the Polish Free Army under Marshal Anders. He leant forward and said: "Do you know who I am?"

I was not pleased. These idiots were trying to browbeat me into allowing them to drive straight into danger - and if they were harmed no doubt I would be blamed. "Sir," I said, "I don't give a damn who you are, you are not going down there." My fellow policeman on the check point had already pulled out his gun, ready to back me up with force if necessary. The high-ranking British officer decided to ignore me, and told his driver to proceed down the road to the right. Seeing this, I raised my tommygun and put two bullets through his tyres.

"Carry on, sir," I said respectfully.

The officer was furious, and asked me where the nearest telephone was. I directed him to the phone used by the nearest Polish regiment, just across the road. In a few minutes he was onto the Polish Provost Marshall, my Commander, to complain. But it did him no good, for the Marshall told him that a man who could not obey his own orders was not fit to give orders in the first place.

One of my last exploits was to advance the Allied Front by fifteen miles in a day, and win a commendation from Headquarters - without meaning to do so.

It was during the battle of Ferrara, and that day I had received written orders from Headquarters to take thirteen men down to the village of Castel St. Pietro to establish a military police checkpoint. The checkpoint was to be set up at 1500 hours on that day. As I arrived at Faenza driving a truck, I found there at Headquarters twelve military policemen all ready to be collected. As soon as I reported, a sergeant named John Wesolowski appeared from HQ (I knew him from Africa; he had been an instructor in Judo and Jujitsu during my training), and as soon as he spotted me, he said laughingly, "When I said goodbye to you in Africa I was hoping that that was the last time I would see you." Then he became serious, and said to me quietly, "To tell you the honest truth, I never thought that you had survived your active mission into Germany, because I never heard a word about where you were." (Security was obviously not as tight as it should have been; he should not have known of my missions.)

I smiled and replied: "Only the good die young; the bad ones live forever." It transpired that he was to come with me. I told the men they were going to Castel St. Pietro, and they began to climb aboard. I then asked John if he knew where Castel St. Pietro was. He said "Vaguely." I asked him, "How the hell do we get there?" for I had hardly heard of it before. He told me to take the road to Bologna, and we would find Castel St. Pietro on the way.

However, before we got there we were stopped, just past Imola, by a military policeman at a traffic control point who told us that the bridge ahead had been blown up and as far as he knew we had to turn right to bypass it. We followed his instructions, and then at the beginning of the detour we came across some traffic on the road, but for fifteen miles after that there was no traffic but ourselves. This made me uneasy; and the rumble of heavy artillery fire which signified the front line was coming from behind us instead of in front of us.

We drove another three or four miles, and heard machine gun fire, and also individual shots, and soon we came in sight of burning buildings; German shells were exploding within a hundred yards on our right. I pulled up behind a large building and got out, with Sergeant John, to investigate the matter, as we had seen some of our soldiers about. We soon learnt that we had gone too far, and that this building was the main storage depot for goods at Ferrara station and the station was on the opposite side of the tracks. Our informant humourously told us that he would not advise us venturing there unless we wished to join the German forces, who were still in occupation there.

We decided to go back and find the road to Castel St. Pietro. As we got into the truck, there between the railway lines we saw front line combat soldiers firing at the Germans. Sergeant John said: "I don't think we could have got any closer to the battle lines." In fact, though we did not know it then, the front line ran through the building near where we left the track; troops in there were firing across the tracks at the Germans, and that building was a priority target for the enemy. We were not near to the front line, we were in it!

As we started driving away from Ferrara towards the main road between Rimini and Bologna, we saw a number of Polish soldiers fighting among themselves in the first village we passed. Since we were, after all, military police, we stopped to sort them out; it was ridiculous that they should be squabbling so near the front line. After questioning them, we found that they had been drinking; they had discovered that a nearby building (outside which they were fighting) was a wine store. While they were drinking, one of the huge barrels had suddenly stopped supplying wine, even though it was still three quarters full. The fight had started then; no doubt one of the idiots had insulted another, or accused them of cutting off the wine, in the usual way with drunken quarrels, completely irrational.

I decided to check up on their story; John and I looked out the wine store, only to find out that they had been telling the truth. Mounting some steps so that I could peer over the edge of the barrel, I asked them to hand me a long wooden gauge, about 3" in diameter, and started moving it about in the wine. The men below shouted up that the wine was flowing again, and I was just about to step down again when I realised that the body of a dead German was floating in the barrel. I immediately passed on this information to Sergeant John, and he tried to dissuade the men from drinking the wine; but to them wine was wine, dead Germans or no, and as soon as we left the storage shed they ran back in again and started drinking all over again.

We did not stop them. Amazingly enough, there is no law against men drinking in the front line. In fact, the soldiers are often encouraged to have a few drinks before going into battle - another fact which is not often emphasised in the official accounts of the war! Also, the men had a right to a drink - it might well be their last. Sergeant John and I just exchanged a smile as we watched them rushing back to the drink - and each knew what the other was thinking. Later, we had a good laugh as we drove away; saying that the body was soaked in alcohol, after all, and therefore disinfected, so there would be no hygiene problem.

About half an hour later, we reached the main road, which ran in a straight line as far as the eye could see. And ten miles further on we ran into a military policeman, who signalled to us to pull in. We asked him what was up, and he simply asked: "Where are you going?" "Castel St. Pietro," said Sergeant John, "there is a sign over there indicating it's only a few yards away." And there was.

"You are in the front line, and ten yards further on the men are in trenches. On the other side of the bridge that has been blown, there are Germans, who blew it up when they were still ten kilometres away on this side." This was a puzzle. Our orders were clear; establish a checkpoint in Castel St. Pietro. I turned to Sergeant John and suggested we check our orders. His orders and mine were both the same, dated the same day, and called for the checkpoint to be established at 1500 hours. It was very nearly that now, and we only had a few minutes to get across the stream to St. Pietro, which was over the bridge.

In spite of the contrary evidence, I trusted my orders. I looked on the other side of the road and saw the white tapes which indicated a clear path through a mine field, and I turned to the policeman and said: "Surely, the bypass has been cleared, because the white tapes are there." He said: "Those are German tapes, our disposal squads have not had a chance to get here yet." However, I decided to go and investigate. As I walked to the other side of the road, he called me to "Duck and run." I listened, but heard nothing, and continued walking, and when I had surveyed the tracks of dust where the Germans had walked when laying the tapes, I decided to walk along the track to the edge of the stream, in spite of a call of warning from my colleagues. I was sure I was safe, however, because I was treading in German footmarks. I looked in the water for mines, and could see no sign of them. Then I checked the other side of the tracks again. Sergeant John asked me what I thought, and I said I felt there were no mines on the road. After more discussion, we decided to carry out our orders, and follow the existing tracks, which I felt were safe. We did so, and crossed over the stream.

Beyond the stream, the road had been tarmaced over, and there were no digging marks on it, so we could proceed with confidence; mines were impossible. And just a few yards beyond was the main street of the village, where we were to set up our checkpoint. As we drove down the narrow street between the buildings on either side, the local inhabitants were looking out of the doors and windows. Noticing our white helmets they called "Americano, Americano," and we realised that they had never seen allied troops before. That was worrying.

The houses were of typical Italian construction, with steps leading down from the front door to the main road, and these made the road narrow. I came to a halt; things felt very wrong. As I did so, German troops showed their faces at the end of the street, pulling at the wheels of a 20mm machine gune which was directed straight at us. No order was given; all the men jumped from the truck and took shelter behind the steps, all in a few seconds.

We were only just in time - the Germans opened fire, the truck disintegrated and blew up, and we were very much part of the front line. We did not have a great deal of combat experience, but we did our best. Everyone of us had a sub-machine gun, and so we had quite a lot of firepower. We blasted away. What we did not know was that the policeman who had tried to stop us advancing had telephoned Polish HQ and told them about us crossing the stream by truck, and that the stream was clear of mines; he also told them that he could hear machine gun fire, so we were obviously in trouble.

We were in a tight spot - when suddenly we heard heavy artillery fire from behind us, and the 20mm gun suddenly blew to pieces. Polish HQ had sent in tanks to save us. After that it was nearly over; the Germans, already on the retreat, with morale low, retreated. When we crawled out from the steps, dazed and quite shaken, I began to worry about being court martialled for disobeying orders. I worried even more when, two days later, I received an order from HQ to report to the Commanding Officer; on the way there I worried more and more about the possibility of a court martial.

However, it was all an anti-climax; the Commanding Officer congratulated me for making a wise decision, and informed me that by my action, the front moved forward along the main road towards Bologna by about fifteen miles that day. He then read out an official commendation which went on my record. Actually, my own opinion was that I should have been punished for putting fourteen men (including myself) in needless danger. However, who was I to argue with High Command's wisdom?

Afterwards, I did some checking up. The whole thing had been caused by a mistaken date on my orders. Some clerk had typed in a date one day in advance of the proper one. The following day, the front would have moved forward to place Castel St. Pietro behind our lines. But I had arrived a day early!

That was my last bit of excitement on active duty. Soon after, I was transferred to an interrogation camp for German prisoners, outside Forli, where I worked under Inspector Slack of Special Branch, whom I already knew quite well, questioning German prisoners and helping to correlate all the information they gave me. But I still had one final surprise to come. It was May 1945, and the war was coming to an end. It was evening, and I was walking along outside the wire fence that bordered the camp, and heard my real name called. Even now, so near victory, we were still cautious, all of us. As for me, I had had caution, wariness and distrust ingrained into me for six years. So I did not respond, but dropped my papers so that I had an excuse to look around.

And there, looking at me through the wire, was Engineer Terjung! Of all the coincidences in my astonishing war career, I think this was the greatest.

I went back to Inspector Slack, my Commanding Officer. (I have not mentioned him before - but I had met him during my Intelligence work. He ranked above my immediate Commanding Officer during the time I was doing my missions, and I met him from time to time. However, during these later times I worked with him directly, and we were on the best of terms.) I asked him if I could see someone in the camp. He was surprised, because it was after 6.00 pm and work had ceased for the day. I explained that it was a personal matter. Normally speaking, the proper procedure was to have a witness present at all interrogations, but he had a date, and wanted to be off. He said that I was free to do as I liked - he trusted me with the prisoners in the daytime, so why not in the evening? So off I went, strolling along the fence, and there was Engineer Terjung, waiting.

He said: "Entschuldigen, mein herr, enschuldigen, Mein Herr."

I said: "Are you calling me?"

He said: "Yes, can I speak to you?: You are so familiar, sir. I knew someone called Maslany, and he was just like you."

I said: "You must be mistaken, my name is Jan Sokolowski. But how can I help you?"

"I want to get in touch with my wife."

I said: "You can't, the Germans are still in control there." And then, of course, he knew it was me, for I knew where his home was.

He said: "Can I talk to you?" I told him to go to the gate, and signed for him to go out. I took him out, told him to remember I was now Jan Sokolwoski, and asked him when he had last seen his wife, Helen. He said that had been just before he joined his unit. He said he had been a Captain in the ordinary German army, but had then been made to join the SS, and was now a Colonel. I asked him after the other Poles in his unit, and he said they were all well, which was true, for it turned out that he had helped many Polish people.

He said if there were any Polish people to be found from the camp which he ran, they would not speak against him. So I put an advert in a Polish soldiers' daily, and within a few days had 20 replies, all willing to speak on his behalf. Of course this made all the difference, and he was well treated.

The wheel had come full circle - first he protected me, and then I was able to help him, even if only in a minor way.

The last thing I have to tell about my war experiences is perhaps the saddest - not for me personally, but for the whole Polish nation.

In April of 1945, there was a very high level meeting between Marshal Anders of the Free Polish Army and others of the Allied High Command. It took place at Rimini Airport, in a large tent. There was a lavish spread of drinks and food. The whole event was guarded by thirty police of all nationalities, but most of them were outside. Inside the tent there were only six - all military police: two Poles, two English, and two Americans. I was one of the two Poles.

The reason for our presence was very simple. Anders was always nervous of his safety. Early in the war, when Stalin had just released him and many other Poles from Russian prisoner-of-war camps, there had been a high level meeting, just such as this, in Southern Russia. There had been a quarrel, and a Russian colonel had pulled a gun, and tried to kill Anders. But a Polish sergeant had been standing behind the colonel, and was quicker than he - and the Russian colonel died with a bullet through the head. (I met the man who did it myself.) After this incident Anders was always rather careful of his safety - I and my colleague were his bodyguards.

The meeting started amicably. There was Anders himself, Montgomery, and an American general, who shall be nameless - and you will soon see why. Anders talked earnestly. He had a very simple request to make - he wanted to see his country free, and he intended to free it himself. He had plenty of men. Apart from the existing Polish divisions, there were many thousands of Poles in German uniforms, conscripts, who were sitting in the Allied prisoner-of-war camps. They would join him at once if asked. All he needed were munitions - tanks, ammunition and planes. With those, he would march straight home across Europe, and kick out the Russians, whom he still (and with good reason) regarded as enemies.

However, he was told that the matter had been settled. A deal had been made - the Russians were to have Poland. Anders was told he was part of the British army, and had to respect this casual disposal of his country - one of the most cynical bits of double-dealing of which I have ever heard.

Anders was furious (he had been drinking heavily, and this made it worse). His rage was really something to see, and in the end the American general just left to avoid the unpleasantness - and maybe also because his conscience pricked him. Montgomery at least had the courage to stay, and calmed Anders down before the meeting ended.

And that was that. The Polish army stopped at Ravenna on the Eastern side of Italy, and inland at Bologna. The only units who went further north were lightly armed police units. A great opportunity was lost, and a whole nation was handed over to the dictatorship which occupies the country to this day. I am sure that many aging politicians now must regret that stupid and wicked arrangement. I, certainly, have never forgotten or forgiven what I heard then.

Chapter 23

AFTERWARDS

And so, that is nearly the end of my story. Shortly afterwards, I arrived in Britain on 24th August 1945. Like all Poles who had served the British, I was told that I was welcome to stay in Britain and help to build the bright new postwar world the politicians promised us. Well, we got it - a bit chipped here and there at the edges, it is true, and not quite the same shape as they said it would be. How true it is about politicians, that one can always tell when they lie, because their lips move. But then, joking apart, they are only mortals, and sometimes things go wrong for them, as for the rest of us. I was demobilised in Birmingham in 1948.

On the whole, I have had a happy and successful life, and have had many adventures since the wartime years. My principal achievement has been to found the first freelance design consultancy in Britain - it opened for business in 1957. They said we would not survive, but we now employ twenty seven men and are still in existence. Engineering has remained my first love; recently, when I was ill and had little to do, I bought broken down TV sets and mended them to amuse myself.

My scars from the war remained, however - the mental scars, that is. The many terrible things I witnessed, and worse still, the terrible things that I was forced to do, have always stayed with me - the more so because I had to cut off my natural feelings for so long, in order to survive. As feelings always do, they returned, and for seventeen years after the war I had constant nightmares. I would wake up screaming, crying, covered with sweat; on many occasions these nightmares repeat themselves, so that I lived over and over again the same sequences of events, concerning the same people, the same landscape. They are so precise that in my dreams I could even identify the rocks, hills and fields where the original action took place. I saw the faces of friends and enemies, and sometimes such dreams would only end as someone pulled a gun on me, and I was about to be killed.

The dreams often concerned the events of my partisan life; but I also dreamt about my missions, and these were even more frightening, because the fear was greater, as it had been in real life. I always woke perspiring and in fear. These dreams lasted until 1961, and had a great effect on my married life, because I constantly interrupted my wife's sleep, which made her cross with me. During the nightmares my body used to shake and my arms would stretch out to get hold of something, and sometimes I have woken holding my wife tightly to me. In the end, this made her afraid and she was worried that I might harm her.

These things never leave you. All over the world, other ex-partisans, prisoners and soldiers must have been waking from their sleep with similar dreams. We are the unseen casualties, who receive no pension and no pity, because people do not even know we exist, and every war leaves us behind, like debris in the street after an accident, unregarded and unthought of.

This book has helped however, helped me at last to write out my experiences and expel them, though I do not expect that I shall ever be free of them entirely. But perhaps I shall sleep more easily.

I have had my share of unhappiness too; partly as a result of my dreams and my behaviour towards her when asleep, my wife's terror of me grew till she went to a psychiatrist, who asked me to come and see him. However, after talking to and examining me, he said it was my wife who needed treatment. She eventually entered a mental home; but made me promise to release her if she asked after seven days. I did so, since I had promised, even though the doctor there felt she needed further treatment; she never returned however, and though we lived together and had a great deal of happiness, she often left unpredictably and for no reason - so maybe the doctor was right. Eventually we divorced, having been married for eleven years.

Since I do not wish to be plagued by treasure hunters, I had better say what happened to the gold I left buried in the mountains in the hole beneath the rock where, later, I starved for twenty-one days: Well, for many years I avoided the place. The premonition of ill fortune which surrounded the gold kept me away. But at last, when I began to write this book, and my co-author, Jeremy, began to ask me questions, I felt a stirring of curiosity, and I went back to Italy. I went to the hillside where I had hidden the bars - and found it greatly changed. There was now an estate of modern houses all over the hillside, once so wild. The German bunkers had vanished.

I found the rock, however, and the hole. But the bodies had gone, as well as the guns we had left there when we escaped. And someone had been digging. Somewhere in Italy, there is a rich man or men, who either followed my tracks at the time and marked the place, or, more likely, just found the weapons and the bodies and made a lucky guess.

I do not care a rap. I have always made money easily with my skills and abilities. Actually, I am glad the gold has gone, and I do not have to worry about it any more. That is the end of that.

What happened to the other people who you have met as you went with me along my lonely journey?

Well, my father, that remarkable man, was killed during the war. He had been organising resistance against the Russians in Poland, and on Good Friday, 1940, he was shot in the central square at Lwow. The funny thing is that I have never accepted the fact of his death. He was a uniquely gifted man, wily, and with a great gift for survival, and at the back of my mind I have always felt that he is still alive. My psychic promptings about imminent death have always been right, so perhaps I am right about this too - but I do not know. Certainly we have never seen him again.

Each of my sisters was raped about fourteen or fifteen times by Russian and German soldiers. However, they are still alive.

My mother survived the war, and the ingratitude and bad treatment of my eldest brother, but is now dead too.

My eldest brother is dead, and I cannot feel sorry for that.

Many of my Polish friends who worked for the Germans later defected to the Russians and joined their cause. Some of them are even now Colonels in the Russian army.

My oldest friend, Roman Zagurski, came through the war relatively unscathed. Having been brought to Italy by the Germans, he worked outside Bologna, then near Ferrara, then Padua, and after on a bridge on the River Po. Towards the end,he managed to find an Italian girlfriend, and hid himself away an Italian farm. In fact, so tucked away was he, he did not even realise that the war had ended! Like me, he is a survivor. He is still very much alive and well, and lives in Birmingham. He has prospered in Britain, but is very much a Pole at heart, and speaks English even worse than my own.

Herr Engineer Terjung also did well for himself - he is now high in the councils of NATO, and a very much respected official, as he deserves to be. He did no more than his duty for his country, and always behaved chivalrously and correctly I am proud that he is still my friend. Incidentally, in case anyone wonders about it, he never held it against me that I escaped from his house - he said that he would have done the same in my place.

Anton and Stefan, the two Russian guards I met in the labour camp, also came to the West, and the last I heard of Anton, he lived in Italy.

Omar, my partisan commander, is now a millionaire, and likes to forget the past. Like most real live wires, he looks always to the future.

So many of my other friends and comrades are now dead. I was very young in those days, and most of them were older than I - and I am far from young any more. So the years have carried them away. Zio is dead now, and so is Inspector Slack of the Special Branch. Many of my partisan friends died during the war and never lived to see the freedom for,which they fought so hard.

Others of course disappeared, or were just lost sight of in the confusion and the whirlwind of conflict. What happened to Vorlamov, my Russian railway friend, and his lovely daughter Maria, my first love? I wish I knew. And the priest who helped me in Florence cathedral, and so many others.

I particularly remember Shannon Berggi, who protected me so well and loved me so dearly in the short time we spent together. After the allied forces had occupied Florence, I found myself there; you will remember that I was in hospital there after returning from my fourth mission. I had already made enquiries about Shannon without success, but then, when I was on the spot, I went out to her house as soon as I could move about, on the same tramlines where we had ridden when I was on the run. I found the house occupied by an Italian Communist organisation. You will remember that Shannon's parents were right wing sympathisers, and the neighbours told me they had moved away towards Milan, in Northern Italy, where they had relatives, with the retreating German forces.

Later, when the war was over, I made more enquiries via British Headquarters. However, they could not trace anyone with Shannon's name in Milan. In 1951, when I was studying in Italy, I advertised in OGGI, the popular newspaper, for news of her, but got nothing. I advertised again in 1961, again with no result Maybe someone will read this book who remembers her If she is still alive, I would very much like to hear from her, or from anyone who knows what became of her.

If this book has any other purpose, it is this. War is so often seen as a matter of patriotism, and gallantry, of inspiring deeds and self-sacrifice. And sometimes it is. Certainly I was myself devoted to the cause of Poland during the war, and happily fought for my country and it's right to live in freedom. Unfortunately, it has not found it yet.

But war has a much uglier and meaner side. and this was the side I saw most of. I saw the way human beings become sadistic beasts. and treat their enemies. who, however bad. are human too. as lower than dirt. I have seen men forget everything but their own needs. shouldering aside others to grab food for themselves.

I also remember the political cynicism and opportunism that flourish especially in wartime. Germany's invasion of Poland, which brought Britain into the war. is remembered. It suited Britain's book at the time to forget and ignore the Russian invasion of Poland which took place at the same time. I have already talked about the Allied cynicism and dishonesty which led to my country being handed over to the dictatorship of the Communists, who practise the imperialism of the Tsars under the crust of a new ideology.

We small band of survivors live on. and remember these things, the side of war that does not go down in the official histories. Such things. to take one small instance. as the Americans shooting their own men during that riot in Rome. And I have decided to set down my memories so that they shall not be lost. If it reminds a few people here and there just how awful and destructive war is. I shall not have wasted my time.